Let's Talk About Race *in* Storytimes

Let's Talk About Race *in* Storytimes

Jessica Anne Bratt

Foreword by Kirby McCurtis

Editions
CHICAGO 2022

JESSICA ANNE BRATT is the director of community engagement and outreach at the Grand Rapids (Michigan) Public Library. She was named a *Library Journal* Mover and Shaker in 2016. She leads facilitations about how to have productive conversations about race in storytime. Although she could tell you many stories about all the ways in which she is involved in Libraryland, the coolest millennial thing for her was having MTV reach out for an interview. She was recently featured on the national radio program *The Takeaway* with Tanzina Vega. When not on the local news trying to convince the world to give libraries a try, she is experiencing her newest adventure: motherhood. Or reading fan fiction.

● ●

© 2022 by Jessica Anne Bratt

Extensive effort has gone into ensuring the reliability of the information in this book; however, the publisher makes no warranty, express or implied, with respect to the material contained herein.

ISBN: 978-0-8389-3789-1 (paper)

Library of Congress Control Number: 2021043149

Book design by Alejandra Diaz in the Rooney and Fieldwork Geo typefaces.
Cover design by Kimberly Hudgins. Cover image ©JungleOutThere/Adobe Stock

♾ This paper meets the requirements of ANSI/NISO Z39.48-1992 (Permanence of Paper).

Printed in the United States of America
26 25 24 23 22   5 4 3 2 1

To
**EVERETT
AND ZOEY,**
my living love letters
to this world

CONTENTS

FOREWORD

Storytime is a key building block to school success. We, who are practitioners of children's services, know that library storytimes and programming for our youngest patrons (birth to age 5) help build social and academic skills that directly correlate to being ready for formal schooling. Using a variety of approaches, we work to ensure that children are learning and can express themselves while their parents and caregivers gain a deeper understanding of what we are doing, why this programming is important for their children's development, and what they can be doing at home to support growth. During storytime we introduce early learning standards in a fun and developmentally appropriate way that helps build language and literacy skills, social and emotional development, motor skills, and basic math concepts.

We live in a society that as a whole teaches children that race is a social category of significance, making informed awareness and regular conversation about race essential for all children but especially for white children who have privilege in the United States because of the color of their skin. Yet so many storytimes do not include this awareness as a concept or skill set that needs to be built and strengthened for children or their parents and caregivers. One of the biggest ways that racism shows up in our own institutions is through silence. Why? I can only guess that the answer is fear, because talking about race with children may not be easy or feel natural. But we know that children are not color-blind, and research shows that children recognize race from a very young age. In "Children Are Not Colorblind: How Young Children Learn Race," Erin N. Winkler, PhD, describes a study that followed two hundred Black and white children from age 6 months to 6 years and found that infants are able to nonverbally categorize people by race and gender at 6 months, toddlers as young as 2 years old use racial categories to reason about people's behaviors, and 3- to 5-year-olds not only categorize people by race but express bias based on race. This research disproves the belief that children only have racial biases if they are directly taught to do so. The need to help children make sense of their categorization, and what that means in a larger societal context, is so important. And not having conversations about race is an unearned privilege that not all people are granted in American society.

So where do we start? Sharing diverse books is a good step, as is bringing children to diverse spaces, but passive exposure is not enough. In *NurtureShock: New Thinking About Children*, authors Po Bronson and Ashley Merryman come to the conclusion that just being in a racially diverse environment is not enough for kids to have better racial attitudes. Children can grow to understand that everyone has a unique experience and that one's race will form their experience, but that understanding requires regular, clear conversation. For library staff who serve youth, storytime is a great venue to begin these conversations with children and their parents and caregivers.

Jessica Bratt is a librarian who has been leading efforts related to the work of talking about race in storytime for years, both in practice and in teaching other library professionals how to begin. In 2018, when I began coteaching a class for parents of preschoolers called "Talking about Race and Racism with Young Children" at Multnomah County Library, I knew she was the one person I needed to connect with. Not only has she been trying out different phrases and approaches for years, she has real-life experience with other practitioners. This was valuable information to share with parents in my class as they did their homework—actually practicing sharing books with their children and talking about race intentionally.

This book is designed to give you practical steps and scripts to ensure that you are talking about race in storytime. Throughout this book, Bratt explores how to approach talking about race with preschool-age children, reveals how you can use picture books as conversation starters, and shares resources that will help continue the dialogue. I highly recommend *Let's Talk About Race in Storytimes*; whether you are just getting started on your antiracism journey or you are a seasoned advocate for equity and inclusion at your library, you will learn something from this book that will help curb your fears about race talks and support self-reflection as you continue to battle the ways in which whiteness and privilege are normalized in our society.

—Kirby McCurtis

PREFACE
The World According to Whimsy

I was born to two parents who were very passionate about their com-munity. They were members of the Black Panther Party, and they were also both teachers. They live on the South Side of Chicago and have stayed in a neighborhood that was nice but was ravaged by the crack epidemic of the 1980s. I grew up talking and learning about race. Our family doctor, Herbert Lerner, worked in the Black Panther Party free clinic and opened his own practice to help reverse the segregated practices whereby Black people could visit the doctor only on one day of the week.

I did not get to this work alone or in an isolated bubble. One thing that is true for me, but that I find is also the case for most of my colleagues of color, is that this work speaks to our families because the policies and laws regarding race affected us so deeply. I stand on my ancestors' shoulders. My parents are from the South, separately moving north as a part of the Great Migration. My dad had to flee the South because of threats to his life, all stemming from race. My maternal grandfather was born in 1898 and had twenty-two children (my mother is the youngest). My paternal grandfather was the only Black man in Grenada, Mississippi, who owned his own land. My parents were the first college graduates on both sides of their families.

My parents graduated high school in the 1960s, which meant that college was their first "integrated" experience. One of the research studies that had a huge influence on my mother and how she parented was the Doll Study (which showed that because of how Black people were portrayed in films and books, children associated darker dolls with being bad). She made sure to instill in my brother and me a love of our history and of our blackness in order to be able to move about in society comfortably in our own skin.

Much of the time, white culture portrays Black people who align or agree with the majority culture as the only acceptable "Black" role models. My parents wanted us to see all different types of Black people.

They took us to museums and other places that showed all types of Black professionals. The DuSable Museum of African American History in Chicago, for example, was highly influential in my learning about Black culture. My parents surrounded us with friends and family to give us positive experiences with a diversity of Black culture. Black people are not a monolith. More importantly, when I started private school and battled against coded words that portrayed Black people as "other," these experiences helped build a foundation of support.

My mother also gave my brother and me dozens of books that showed the vast array of blackness and Black culture. We read about the popular African Americans in history such as Martin Luther King Jr., Rosa Parks, and Frederick Douglass, but my parents also made sure that we read about many more examples of Black excellence (including Marcus Garvey, W. E. B. Dubois, Elizabeth Keckley, Ida B. Wells, Gwendolyn Brooks, Nina Simone, Angela Davis, Fred Hampton, Malcolm X, James Baldwin, and Shirley Chisholm, just to name a few). My mother told us that mainstream society would show us one thing, but that Black people can do—and have done—all things.

By the time my parents had me, they had slowed down a bit. They were in their 40s when I could make memories, and their activism came mostly through church. Thinking it would help, they also put me in private school. At my private school, I was one of the few Black kids. All my teachers were white. The nice way to say it would be that they were insensitive to race and diversity. The honest way to say it would be that they were racist. For example, my history teacher excluded me from the "Family History" project because he said there was no way I could know. When I told my parents, they responded that this was good training for me and for the world I'd be entering. This world wouldn't solve my problems for me.

But they also wanted me to know my own history, which definitely wasn't taught in school. To make up for what wasn't taught in my school, my parents gave me books about African Americans being excellent in their work and used the summers for a different kind of education. We'd visit museums and examples of Black excellence around Chicago.

I am bubbly by nature, loud, passionate, and will (and often do) talk at length about libraries, equity, and race. Libraries are limitless because they touch every aspect of society. They are the equalizer in a world where public infrastructure is quickly crumbling. Librarians can provide knowledgeable conversations rooted in science that can help conquer ignorance and fear. Books and libraries shaped the way I see and interact with the world, beginning when I was very young. I learned how to walk when I was 7 months old and would sneak out of my crib and eavesdrop on the adults. I wouldn't sleep and could never get my brain to stop moving. My mom, who needed a bit of a break, turned me on to books. There was a rule that during nap time and at bedtime, I didn't *have* to sleep, but I couldn't leave the room. So I'd lie there and read. I see now, as an adult, how foundational books were to my growth and to my understanding of the world, and the deep impact they have made on my views of equity, diversity, and inclusion (E/D/I). For me, this work is a natural outflow of my passions, skills, and areas of interest.

I loved libraries so much that I've always worked at them. My first job, at 16, was as a librarian. I started out as a page at the South Shore branch of the Chicago Public Library, which was about six blocks from my house. The librarian, Ms. Dorothy Evans, made a big impression on me. She seemed to know everything. She could answer any question I could think of. If I was curious about something, I could turn to her. There were books about everything! She took me under her wing. She is the reason why I'm a librarian. She did something *so* special, which I hope to replicate one day. She gathered all of her "best" library kids and brought us to the Coretta Scott King Book Awards Breakfast Banquet. She introduced me to a whole other layer of librarian work outside the building. She is the reason why libraries, to me, are limitless. Black professionals know how hard it is to navigate the workforce. Intergenerational mentorship is important in making sure that kids are able to see representations of themselves in a *big* way.

One other thing that played a major role in my development, and that I'd thought of as a sidenote until recently, is my love of music. After books and libraries, music is my number two passion. I have played the piano my whole life and took piano lessons and played in competitions throughout my childhood. (Before becoming a librarian, I actually thought I would do something with music.) In music, one thing that is of fundamental import is that you must practice in order to succeed. Although that sounds obvious, no piece of music just appears. Anyone who plays an instrument will tell you that you don't get it perfect on the first try. You miss notes and make mistakes every time. The best musicians are very talented, but they're often the ones who have put in the most work. This is true of talking about race in storytime as well. When music comes together, each instrument brings its own flavor. In an orchestra, each piece is vital. Take one out, and you lose the benefit of the collective. It is a celebration of diversity in its purest form. Things that are different come together to make beauty. Each instrument is uniquely shaped and patterned to make that instrument sound the best it possibly can. This uniqueness matters. Music taught me acceptance, practice, and viewing my part as contributing to the collective. Most importantly, music teaches you that "feeling of belonging." You can have all these different, wonderful instruments that are able to harmonize as one beautiful sound. Which is something I've taken with me into the library world.

I tell you this to emphasize that this work is fundamental to who I am. Music and books and libraries are at the core of me. Being an activist was an expectation from my childhood. The goal was always to make the world a better place. So that's what I'm trying to do, in my field of choice, each and every day. We Have to Do More.

As a Black professional, I have always talked about race and diversity when planning and implementing my own storytimes. The work of E/D/I is very natural to me, and I thought it was something everyone did. I quickly found out it was not.

At the time, I was the branch manager of a library on the north side of Grand Rapids, Michigan. I was hosting two storytimes each week. I've always talked about race and diversity during storytimes and would celebrate them. I didn't realize this approach was unique. Patrons noticed and appreciated it and asked me how they could do likewise. I realized after talking with several white staff members that they wanted to help make the world "more equitable" but did not know how.

One example that always stands out in my memory happened during an early literacy committee meeting. One of my colleagues was near retirement, reflecting on her career, and she asked if there was something *more* that librarians should be doing. After all her years of effort, she was seeing that the world was not necessarily changing for the better. We were watching our families struggle with the upheaval caused by misinformation, bullying, and a general lack of empathy.

I started experimenting with the storytimes, which came naturally to me, as a way that I could help my white colleagues feel comfortable engaging with race and providing tools to help disrupt bias at a young age. After dozens of people reached out to me for tips and information, I decided to take a bigger approach. I created the first *Let's Talk About Race in Storytimes* in the fall of 2016. I saw a need that was much larger than simply the branch I was managing at the time, and the need to talk about this subject extended beyond racial and other normal categories. That approach is what you have in your hands.

But since 2016, a lot more people have reached out to me about what to do. This deeply affects all of us and our entire community. Heather McGhee stated it best: "It costs us so much to remain divided . . . I believe it's time to reject that old paradigm and realize that our fates are linked. An injury to one is an injury to all."[1] Talking about race is sensitive because of fear. I want to help people overcome their fears and encourage them to do the work themselves. Silence doesn't bring progress. So I created a tool kit that helps you begin wherever you are. I have a positive outlook on life, and at the core, I'm an optimist. I'm also a nerd. I love video games, fantasy, and fan fiction, and I have a wild imagination. Part of what attracts me to fantasy, science fiction, and everything nerd is the ability to create "new" worlds. Racial equity work requires curiosity and imagination, which translates to my love of all things nerd. So, the training I've presented incorporates those features. To be an agent of change for the world, you have to start with your own self. This includes using your areas of interest, but it also means taking care of yourself. It's hard to heal others if you're starting from a place of brokenness. To get the best results from this book and to do this work to the best of your abilities, you must be healed. We all have bias, we all come through life with traumas, and it is hard to do E/D/I work from a place of pain or cynicism. So join me, as we go through how to talk about race, which starts at home.

It quickly became apparent that people had not implemented, and did not know how to implement, E/D/I in their work. One of my librarians spoke to the fear in a good way. I was encouraging her to celebrate diversity in her storytimes. She had sat through all my trainings regarding talking about race in storytimes. Her anxieties were high, particularly if she had to talk about something sensitive and especially in the current political climate. Her fears were heightened by the fact that the families in attendance were diverse. Such fears are common.

She told me that the first time she made an effort to address diversity, an African American father was with his children, and she saw him tense up. Though she was afraid, she went ahead with her storytime. After it ended, he approached her and thanked her for talking about race in such a positive, informative way. Processing the event afterward, I joked, "He was afraid you were going to say something stupid, because that's what happens so often!" After this experience, she got more comfortable. And once she got more comfortable, it only got better. I've found this is the experience a lot of white people have in mixed spaces. It is a truly beautiful thing to see all parts of society coming together around reading and learning. It is one of the ways that libraries are actively righting wrongs that we were a part of creating.

NOTE

1. Heather C. McGhee, "Racism Has a Cost for Everyone," TED, video, 14:12, December 2019, https://www.ted.com/talks/heather_c_mcghee _racism_has_a_cost_for_everyone?language=en.

ACKNOWLEDGMENTS

AHHHHHH!!! I wrote a book! An actual book. MOM, I WROTE A BOOK! Thank you for having me and pouring into me positive racial identity and giving me the foundational skills and resilience to navigate life. To my life coconspirator and favorite author, Tom, you are the most supportive and generous spouse. I appreciate all your help in editing and helping with the narrative to make sure it reads well. You are the best! Thank you, Jamie Santoro, for contacting me and believing that this work has an official and formalized place in this world.

To growing up at the South Shore Library and working among Black excellence, thank you.

Cheers to my big brother, Joseph, and to all the talks we have about solving all the world's problems, especially about race. To my play sisters, Jeanessa and Misti, y'all have poured into me and given me so much, I will forever be grateful. To my Black gaming sister, Neo, keep bursting into gaming spaces and fighting the good fight for representation and full personhood of every beautiful thing that blackness is. Thank you to my sister-in-law Jenny for talking to me about race and letting me engage in race talks with her kids. Also, my other sister-in-law Sarah who always has a book recommendation handy.

Mia Henry and Elon Cook Lee, y'all are the most phenomenal women. You both met me as a diamond in the rough and helped me shine. Y'all are the epitome of Nikki Giovanni's "Ego Tripping." Y'all are Maya Angelou's "Still I Rise"—Elon Cook Lee, I remember the friend crush I had on you with those gold shoes. I was blown away by your brilliance in handling matters of race. Mia, the way you pivoted in a pandemic and are carving out space with Freedom Lifted is so great to witness.

I will be forever indebted to and humbled by Amita Lonial, Sarah Lawton, and Amy Sonnie for reaching out to me before this work was realized. Thank you to the people at work who made space in giving this work a chance to eventually blossom. Thank you, Marcia

Warner and Lizzie Gall. To people who at one point in time allowed me to talk to them at length about this work, thanks, Betsy Zandstra and Liz Sterling.

Monica and Jenna, we started out at the bottom as baby librarians and now we are here (aka besties). Thanks for always having my back, supporting me, and just being the best friends a girl could ask for. Loa, thank you for partnering with me on a whole new community endeavor while I had a whole book thing going on and a tiny baby. Shine on.

ALL MY CONFERENCE COUSINS: KIRBY MCCURTIS, DR. NICOLE COOK-SMITH, DEIMOSA WEBBER-BEY (THERE ARE MORE OF Y'ALL AND Y'ALL KNOW WHO YOU ARE)—I LOVE YOU ALL. Here's to a brighter and more just world because y'all are in it fighting *all* the good fights.

INTRODUCTION
Why I Started Talking About Race in Storytime

In the summer of 2016, with the deaths of Alton Sterling and Philando Castile, the country was hit by the fact that things are unequal. It was not new, but these deaths were caught on film, broadcast around the world. They were all over social media, and everyone was adding their own commentary. There was a tension that you could feel and a conversation that had turned national. The tension took many forms, ranging from discomfort to rage. Many African Americans call this feeling "Black Pain." I felt it very personally. Philando Castile reminded me of my brother, and what happened to him could have, and has, happened to my family members in the past. In the aftermath of these deaths, I could not sit idly by. I could not be silent in my own life and work space.

On the national level, the conversation centered on awareness. African Americans were all over the place sharing our experiences with police and jobs and authority, and the common theme was that things are not equal. It was very obvious that "the American experience" is very different for minorities than it is for the mainstream. As minorities, we know this. This inequity is part of life for us. From a very young age, we're told to be "twice as good," and we're aware that any interaction with police could turn deadly. Consequently, African American parents have to have "The Talk" with their children, beginning when those children are very young. The Talk is about how to handle the police and what to do when you get stopped because—as Philando Castile and Alton Sterling showed all too clearly—any interaction *could* turn deadly.

The national conversation about awareness is a starting point, but what we want is equity. There had been some movement and progress on this front, headed by organizations like Black Lives Matter. The Black Lives Matter movement began in 2013 as a response to the acquittal of Trayvon Martin's murderer, with the goals of making changes in policy and making our society more equitable.

In the summer of 2016, I waited to see if my industry would take a stand in defense of Black lives. After seeing nothing in my own industry concerning the issues of Black Lives Matter, violence against Black bodies, and issues regarding race and equity, I knew I had to act. One of the things I found inspiring with #blacklivesmatter was their call to use your own expertise to help the movement. So I and a few other librarians started an organization called Libraries4BlackLives. It was our response to the Black Lives Matter movement, our attempt to make things more equitable in the world of libraries. The goal was to help gather collective energy around helping people wake up to the call for a more equitable society, using the tools we knew: books and libraries. Or, as I like to think of it, trying to figure out how to best fight inequalities by using your own superpowers.

I am a doer by nature, so I found the approach of using your own expertise very empowering and realized that engaging in this work was my superpower. It felt freeing. For some people, the answer lies in organizing and protesting; for others, it may be seeking to change and advocate for policy. For me it was taking note of what we have yet to rectify by working in a public library. Throughout the years, public libraries have become more than just information repositories. We are now a community hub or, to quote Eric Klingberg, "palaces of the people" where everyone should feel a sense of belonging. In this case, *everyone* meant representation for all people. All too often in the library world, BIPOC are excluded from this representation.

I began a very personal introspection of how I interacted with the families in my storytimes and how race played a direct part in my creation of storytime sessions. For me, a focus on representation was very natural. I'd always done it—it had been instilled by my mother (an early reading specialist). As a youth services librarian, I knew that a sense of belonging begins at an early age, but so does bias. We need to combat this pattern. People wanted resources. They wanted to understand. They wanted to take action. But they also didn't know where to look. One part of the problem is that in some ways, there is much information and many resources, while in others, there's not enough. There's also the question of what to trust. What to use. What is good? I realized that my knowledge is what I could contribute.

The process led to an action plan that led to lists and blogs and speakings and trainings. What I saw at my own library—but also through conversations on Twitter, with family members, and at library conferences—was that though they knew there was a need and a desire to change the narrative, people didn't know how to do it. It was interesting to hear people process. They were afraid. They felt unequipped. A lot of white people didn't know if they *could* talk about race. But if fear is your narrative, then nothing happens. So I used my superpower and developed a training called "How to Talk About Race in Storytime."

What you're holding is the book version of those training sessions. I intentionally crafted my trainings to be *facilitations* (defined as "the act of helping other people deal with a process"). I like to be interactive (which you'll soon find out), and I like to draw on my audience's experience. My goal is to create a space for reflection, growth, and change. I believe the best in people and think that with guidance we can all do well. In turn, this book is meant to be interactive. The art of anti-racist/anti-bias practices requires work. All the collected knowledge in the world will not help you move forward on your journey if you do not take a step. Self-work is the first step needed to engage in this work to bring it to the community around you. You will find worksheets and questions of reflection that are intended to help you talk about race in a way that is affirming and comfortable for children.

We're hearing more and more that the quest for equity and justice is still current news. Four hundred years of slavery did not end in one day. A more equitable world will not come about simply from reading this (or any) book, but we can help bring about a better world by talking about race with our children. Equity starts at home. We're all at different points of our journey, and that is okay. What you do is take a step forward today, another one tomorrow. By doing so, we can move the world forward, and inch the needle toward the arc of justice and equity.

The Time Is Now

In the summer of 2020, Black Lives Matter protests happened in all fifty states in response to the murders of George Floyd and Breonna Taylor. Talks from these protests centered on systematic oppression, which extended to many systems of society. With an election on the horizon, the protests carried an extra weight that summer. People were commenting about the events everywhere, but one Tweet really caught my eye: "Ruby Bridges is only 65." Ruby Bridges is a civil rights icon who became famous for being the first African American to desegregate the public schools in New Orleans. The first. She's only 65.

Not talking about race has consequences. One of them is that historic events can sound like they're part of the past, rather than the present. Ruby Bridges is a great example of this. She and other students who also desegregated schools are praised in books in elementary schools and taught about in history books, which can have the effect of making the kids who hear about the events think they happened a long time ago. But the fact is that Ruby is younger than many of these same kids' grandparents. Ruby Bridges is the same age as my mother-in-law. Ruby Bridges could easily be one of the grandparents at an elementary school grandparents' day.

A lot of white people are facing what is happening and thinking it's new. It is not. As author and activist Adrienne Maree Brown said, "Things are not getting worse, they are getting uncovered."[1] A few hours and Google can show you countless stories of injustice. In Georgia, after historic turnout by African American voters, the state government is trying hard to suppress the vote. This response is what has always happened. We need action to counter this. Once you see, you cannot unsee, and the question is what do you do about it. That's the much more important question. This is some of that uncovering.

This work is important because we are going to set up the next generation of public servants, law enforcers, and tech designers to either reinforce biases or get better at disrupting them. A *New York Times* video talks about implicit bias being "the fog we all breathe in"[2] and that can shape our split-second reactions rooted in tolerance or intolerance (why not root them in empathy instead?). If we want the next generation to be more loving, more kind . . . to be *actually diverse,* we need to teach those qualities. The truth is, not talking about race and diversity has gotten us to the place we are in now. I want to be like Fred Hampton, who wanted to fight identity oppression with identity solidarity.

The journey can seem overwhelming because of the amount of information out there. There's so much to learn and take in that we can sink into inaction. But inaction leads to more death, more bias, and more inequality. This is why I found such inspiration in the Black

Lives Matter push to use your own area of expertise as the starting point for action. My personal action was to encourage people to believe that they can talk about race and diversity and do so without fear. I'm a positive, encouraging person. So when I take action, it comes from this place. As you go through this book, do not shame yourself for past storytimes or lack of representation. Start now, today. And if you have to atone for past actions, do so. Use the Anti-Racist Action Plan to start thinking about what will be needed to put your learning into action.

ANTI-RACIST ACTION PLAN

1 Think

How do you learn best? Is it by thinking, reading, watching, or listening?

2 Plan

Do self-learning about the identity of blackness.

3 Do

Ask your institution (supervisor, management, etc.) if there is support for learning more about equity, diversity, and inclusion. What programs could you or staff members attend locally or nationally regarding anti-bias practices for children?

One final example before diving in is that of Pearl Townshend. When she was 17, she lived in Raleigh, North Carolina, which had segregated libraries. Pearl had to study at the Black library. She needed a book that the Black library didn't have, so she went to the white library to find a copy. When she tried to enter the library, staff members told her she wasn't allowed inside. She explained her situation and was "allowed" to enter the library, but hidden in the basement. The experience was so traumatic for Pearl, and she felt so unwelcome, that she didn't get a library card until 2015, when she was 90.

Since Pearl's experience, libraries have stepped up to be a part of the solution. Libraries should be places of equity and help. That's what libraries have done. We used to exclude. But after the death of Michael Brown in 2014, when schools were closed down and children didn't have access to materials, the Ferguson (Missouri) libraries opened their doors to the students and were the place they needed. As you read, and throughout this work, pay attention to your emotional and physical state. I have included some helpful tips for processing stressful information.

PROCESSING STRESSFUL INFORMATION

✓ **Tension in the Body**

Oppression is felt in the body. As you work through learning or unlearning history and exploring race, keep in mind how your body is feeling and the emotions that you are experiencing.

✓ **Strong Emotions**

Identify the strong emotions you are experiencing. Unpack them. Is it shame? Guilt? Anger? Denial? Frustration?

✓ **Breathing Techniques**

Learning breathing techniques is essential for processing stressful information. You cannot do this work if you are not emotionally or mentally healed.

It Starts at Home

As an industry, we know how important representation is. Through studies by Lee and Low or the formation of We Need Diverse Books, fighting status quo publishing trends is finally making headway nationally. More libraries are now actively taking audits of their collections and seeing whether they are curating books to represent our identities. This is a good thing.

We know from research that white parents do not talk to their kids about race. Libraries can help combat this deficiency. We can provide tools and build confidence, but we can also model representation. How do we bridge the gap and help parents feel confident about having "check-in conversations about race"?

This discussion about awareness is important. Research has shown that bias begins at about 36 months of age. Humans naturally categorize things, which is very normal and doesn't have to be bad. But when they're steered in a way to categorize some things as better and some worse, that's where the problem begins. The problem plays out by saying that one group of people and their culture are inherently superior and that other identities are subservient or less than that culture.

E/D/I and representation are really important work that starts at home. Kids are resilient and inquisitive, and they notice differences in skin tone, gender, and levels of ability. When they ask questions, be honest. If you don't know, say things like, "I don't know," or "That's a really good question," or "Let's figure that out together." As a caregiver, you might begin this work by quickly scoping your books. Ask questions such as these: Do the characters in your books look the same, or do they look different? Are you reading stories that include different genders and gender identities, races and ethnicities, and cultures that are not your own? Doing so is a great way to start the process of talking about race and diversifying your storytime.

It shows up subliminally, right? When you went into the library, you could see and name the few Black authors published at the time. All those authors were on the Coretta Scott King Book Awards list. There were a few up-and-coming Black authors to be found in the newly created young adult section (Jacqueline Woodson and Angela Johnson), but throughout my schooling, all the characters in the books we read who weren't slaves or servants or workers were white.

As many of us were forced to discover while living through a pandemic, belonging is very important and is going to be more important post-pandemic. The beauty of this work is that it doesn't stop just because the world stops. I did a training session for a museum in Rhode Island wanting to better engage in this work and asked participants what compelled them to do this work when everything was shut down. They said they wanted to be ready to hit the ground running as soon as society opened up. This time is perfect to dig deep into practicing, learning, and getting ready to "hit the ground running" once you can start seeing your wonderful community again in person.

The book you have in your hands is adapted from live training I do on how to talk about race in storytimes. Step into this topic with me, and we can begin to do our part to create a more equitable society.

○○○ SELF-REFLECTION ○○○

Charlene Carruthers, one of the founding members of the Black Youth Project 100 and a well-known queer Black activist and organizer, says the work of E/D/I cannot be done unless you first are able to answer the following questions. Take a moment to answer them for yourself.

> Who am I?

> What are my self-interests?

> Who are my people?

> Who am I accountable to?

> What am I best positioned to do?

> How was I taught Black history? Black history is an integral part of US history. Black people have been integral to shaping the country in terms of the economy, culture, food, fashion, and labor. Often Black history is taught as a subtext or an afterthought. It is not. It is foundational. Knowing Black history enriches one's knowledge of American history.

> How was Black history taught to me as a child, as an adult, or both?

> What famous Black figures do I know?

> Thinking about US history from 1619 to the present, what enslaved narratives do I know? Harlem Renaissance? Reconstruction? Great Migration? Black Power?

> Within those narratives, what intersectionality exists?

NOTES

1. Adrienne Maree Brown, Twitter, July 9, 2016, 11:24 a.m., https://twitter.com/adriennemaree/status/751799298791211008?lang=en.

2. Saleem Reshamwala, "Peanut Butter, Jelly and Racism," New York Times, video, 2:26, December 16, 2016, https://www.nytimes.com/video/us/100000004818663/peanut-butter-jelly-and-racism.html.

THEY SEE RACE

One time when I was working at the public service desk, a coworker and I discussed our introduction to race as kids. I told her that I attended an all-white kindergarten. In kindergarten, the big deal was inviting people to your birthday party. I was invited to many birthday parties, and my mom drove me far into the suburbs and neighboring towns in Indiana to attend these parties. When it was time for my birthday, I went to the store with my mom, spent a long time picking out invitations I liked, and made one for each kid in my class. Excitedly, I went to school the next day and handed out the invitations to my birthday party at my house. Soon after, one by one, my classmates started telling me they couldn't come. Finally, one of my classmates let me in on the secret. He told me no one would be attending my birthday party because I lived in Chicago—"in a bad neighborhood." I remember staunchly defending (as kids do) the people on my block, telling my classmate that my neighbors were nice and that it wasn't bad where I lived. I could not understand. I had never seen a gun or heard gunshots. Every house on our block had a nice lawn.

When I got in the car after school, I was visibly heated. My mom asked what was wrong, so I told her what had happened and asked her what it meant that I lived in a bad neighborhood. I can still picture her grip on the steering wheel, as she tried to explain it to me. She had to explain that a lot of times when Black people live together in a city or urban area, because of how that area is portrayed on the news or in the paper, white people interpret it as a "bad neighborhood." It was my first introduction to the fact that because I looked different, people treated me differently. And also that—in their opinion—this difference was not a good thing. I could not grasp the concept of being thought of as different because I thought that I was the same.

My coworker didn't have anything similar. She'd never thought about race. I've found that this disparity is not unique as I have navigated conversations about race at work. Often, coworkers are shocked when they hear this or other stories from me or other minorities. To us, race is something we're aware of from a very young age. It's something that we have to deal with and navigate constantly. A close friend of mine, Elon Cook Lee, director of interpretation and education in the Historic Sites Department at the National Trust for Historic Preservation, demonstrates this gap quite well in her facilitations. (I was able to attend the Cultural Heritage and Social Change Unconference led by Jon Voss.) She asks participants to write down their earliest memory of race and then line up by that age on a timeline. The results are always the same. People of color are lined up in the front, whereas our white counterparts are often in high school and beyond before they're ever aware of their racial identity.

A lot of this disparity is intentional. It's taboo to talk about race, and consequently the subject is avoided. Minorities are left to deal with it while society attempts to move beyond racial lines. A term often used for people claiming to be "woke" or "not racist" and therefore open to diversity is *color-blind*. The term is intended to convey that such people do not see race when they think about people. It can come with additional comments about being beyond race or post-racial. Their assumption is that being color-blind is a good thing because when you don't think in terms of race, you don't think *negatively* based on someone's race. But the problem with this line of thinking is that it goes against what humans do, while also unintentionally devaluing the person of color.

At the end of the day, a lot of "color-blind" talk is loaded with coded words for race. After the civil rights movement, politicians have used these coded—and often derogatory—words instead of explicitly mentioning race. Words like *urban* or *inner-city* are used to describe the specific parts of the city where minorities live. When a Black-issues protest is organized, the protestors are described as "thugs" or "illegal immigrants." Contrast these terms to the words *patriot* or *middle class* that white Americans use to think about and describe themselves. This type of coded language has helped adults avoid having discourse and healthy conversations about race. According to Ian Haney López, author of *Dog Whistle Politics: How Coded Racial Appeals Have Reinvented Racism and Wrecked the Middle Class*, "It allows people to say, 'Hey, I'm just criticizing the behavior, not criticizing a racially defined group.'"[1]

A lot of the time, because of the loaded term *racist* nowadays, white people are fearful of talking about race. As a result, problems that stem from race persist while some people think we're beyond it. Other women in positions of power often demonstrate this situation quite well. "Do you face more discrimination," one such woman asked me, "because of your race or gender?" "Race," I responded quickly. "Really?" she said, genuinely surprised. "I thought it would be gender." In her mind, society had moved past race, becoming color-blind, but had not moved past gender. This happens because you cannot avoid gender but can "other" race through coded language. Most people want to hear from someone who has had that lived experience, yet a lot of times when someone shares their vulnerabilities, white listeners may not affirm the experience of oppression but, instead, say that the speaker has a victim mentality from it.

For Black people, and other minorities, race comes into play very often in ways that white people do not experience. For example, when I was first hired as a youth services librarian, I was told that I was hired only because the administration liked Black people. Most of the time when Black people are in a predominantly white space, they have to stay quiet because they represent their whole community and do heavy lifting on defending cultural nuances of the ways that Black people think, act, or live. Many white people have few friends of color, so the one or two whom they know end up representing the whole group. Most of the time Black people *do not* get the privilege of being individuals. We are considered a group. This code switching is not unique to BIPOC. I remember my mom letting me know that when I went outside, I had to make sure to act a certain way and not be threatening to white people because I may be their only interaction with Black people.

Artist and entrepreneur Kenyatta Forbes got tired of being a "Black ambassador" in white spaces, so she invented a game called Trading Races to get adults of *all* races to talk through their biases, both conscious and unconscious, about the identity of blackness. I really like the game, which deals with this issue quite well.

The game consists of a stack of cards with pictures of people of different races and genders. Each participant gets five cards. You ask a question like, Who's the blackest?, and each person goes through their cards, laying down the one they choose and explaining their reason, which is where things get interesting. At the end of the round, the group must come to consensus about who is the "blackest." The game is supposed to be fun, which a lot of people have a hard time leaning into. The conversations that come up are almost always interesting, especially because not all the cards picture people with black skin. There are a lot of controversial figures—Clarence Thomas, Tiger Woods, Eminem, Rachel Dolezal, Stacey Dash, and Bill Clinton, for example.

Let's take Bill Clinton as a case in point. Some people call him the first Black president. They talk about what he did for the Black community, *but* he also created the three-strikes law, which dispro-portionately oppresses Black people. To this day, there are people in jail simply for a third strike. What is worth more? What makes more of an impact? The group must decide.

I played this game with my coworkers before using it in training. A lot of people are nervous the first round or two because talking about race is uncomfortable. It highlights a lot of what we do badly and fear in our society. We will never as a society get better at discussing "taboo" topics, much less raise the next generation to be a tolerant society, if we cannot unpack blackness. First, the game shows others in the group whether you were taught any Black history or know Black pop culture. Then it adds layers as you engage with other players in trying to "out-Black" other characters. This conversation leads to dis-cussions about physical differences, achievements, intersectionality, social inequality, power, and more.

Kenyatta Forbes was attempting to create a space in which people could talk about race. I love my Black peers across the nation because most have fun with the game. There will always be some Black people who take personally this attempt to identify "blackness" because of all the trauma it brings up, and there will be white people who want to use it as an excuse in this new culture to not "practice" wokeness because "they are not the experts on race." I point out that we are all "experts" on race (a lot of time the wrong things about race). Whenever white people go out in society and have an interaction, or see a group of people coming into the library and do not give them the same experience based on assumptions, they are leaning into their expertise about race. Talking is the key to the game, and you cannot play without dialogue. When you play this game, you enter a space that is not black and white, literally and metaphorically. This game is not about winning; it is about how we are all losers because we do not have conversations about the malleability of race. When we do not know our full history that incorporates *all* Americans and our achievements and when we act as if only Black people need to know, then this ignorance affects all of us.

The game does a great job of highlighting that "race" is not clear or well defined. The concept has been shaped and modeled and used to oppress from the first caste system (which originated in Spain) to the science and laws in America. Race is tied into the very economics of our nation in the form of chattel slavery and in creating policies to pit Indigenous people, indentured servants, and the enslaved populations against each other. Race is many things, but one thing it is not is color-blind. This is because people are not color-blind. In our nation, opportunity has been doled out and defined and allowed *by* and *because of* race. People of color have been on the receiving end of the negatives of this opportunity. I've heard my husband, who is white and has ancestors who were immigrants, speak to this. When talking about opportunity, a lot of his relatives mention that they're descendants of immigrants who have had to work hard and struggle to make it. He responds to them by saying that because of their Dutch heritage, they were able to blend in with the dominant culture. And he points out that the Indigenous people who were already here were pushed to reservations, while African Americans were brought here against their will. So when mainstream society says "color-blind," it ignores all past oppression and essentially wants to wipe it clean. This is not helpful.

The main danger is that by being color-blind, we make all people the same. When we make all people the same, we assume that one set of norms works for all people. We think that one set of rules, one system of judgment, one system of evaluation is good enough to cover the masses, but it's not. Different cultures value things differently. "Loud" to one culture is normal to another. Time is valued very differently by different cultures. When the dominant culture creates the system based on what *it* values, the result is systemic racism. What happens is that those in positions of power make the rules, systems, and evaluations, and it's up to the rest to assimilate or get steamrolled. Our modern society is now seeing that the system does not work for everyone. We ask, What do we do? How do we respond? But such questions have always been part of the conversation. Think of the famous Frederick Douglass speech: "What, to the American slave, is your 4th of July?" Think about how, after the Civil War, Black liberation was allowed to blossom during the Reconstruction period and then the Black Codes and Jim Crow laws were introduced.

Sometimes it's easier to explain concepts with fictional characters than with real people, so I'll use my favorite superhero (other than Storm), Groot. I love superheroes and comics, and one of my absolute favorites is *Guardians of the Galaxy*. It's a blend of everything I like, and the characters make everything fun, especially as they're doing their part to save the universe—which is what librarians do every day! When we meet Groot in *Guardians of the Galaxy*, his first words are "I am Groot." His next words are "I am Groot." Same for his next line and his next line and his next. The other characters, like the audience, understandably are frustrated. They say to him, "Why do you keep saying that?" or "We heard you already." They're expressing what many viewers also wonder—why does this character say only this one thing? Does he not know how to talk? But then, very soon after, we find out from Rocket, who can understand Groot, that Groot is a tonal language and is, in fact, one of the most expressive languages in the entire universe, though it uses only three words. When you know this, you can recognize that *I am Groot* is much different than *I. am. Groot.* Which is much different than *I AM Groot* or *I AM GROOT!* and so on. Once we know how the language works, we can appreciate what the language Groot brings to all language.

Groot is a good example of the danger of color blindness. When viewed from the position that language functions only one way (color-blind), and that one way is only through words, it is easy to assume that a language of three words is very limited. Viewed from the uniquenesses of the language, it then becomes about appreciation, which is one thing so many of us love about comic books in general. Sometimes superheroes are a good example of what society should look like *because* there is no stigma attached. No one can look at Drax, Star-Lord, Rocket, or Gamora and talk about their own ancestry, origin story, or political opinions. We just appreciate these characters. The diversity adds to the joy. For a lot of people, it's easier to appreciate this diversity in fiction, but it is possible to do so in real life, too. We just have to teach appreciation, and then life can be as fun as comic books!

Children Notice Differences

When I found out I was pregnant, one of the first things I got excited about was reading to my child. My spouse laughed at me the first time he saw me reading to our son, the third night after coming home from the hospital. The first book we read was Margaret Wise Brown's *Goodnight Moon*. My mom, a reading specialist, had read the book to me when I was young, so I continued the tradition. *Goodnight Moon* is great for growth and development. The book begins with a two-page spread showing a complete room, before describing the specifics of what's in the room on the next two pages. This cycle repeats until you name every item in the room. Then, using the same pattern and repetition, you begin the process of saying good night to each of those items.

It was fun to see my own son begin unpacking the book at different developmental stages. As he developed, he noticed more on his own, including a (fun) mouse that appears throughout the book. Although the room stays the same, the mouse moves all around. It's on a shelf on one page, on the bed on the next. Our son started to point to the mouse on each page. Kids enjoy books like this because they help them observe the world around them. The mouse demonstrates that in the midst of the routine, children notice change. Our son is 3 now, so *Goodnight Moon* is no longer in his evening routine. But though the books have changed, the pattern recognition and processing of the world have not. One of the books we've been reading for the past year or so is Michael Tyler's *The Skin You Live In*. The book is a celebration of hues and pigmentation. At its core, the book is a celebration of diversity, with characters of all different skin tones. All children will be able to identify themselves, which I've seen them do firsthand. We live very close to my son's cousins, who are white, and read the book together. When we read it to the children, they point to the characters in the story that look like them and call them their own names. The white boy is Anson, the white girl is Norah, and the Black boy is Everett. They also do this for the adults in the book. They'll point to the different characters and call them by our friends' and relatives' names, based on each character's skin tone. (Everett points to one and says "Aunt 'Nessa.") The children do this not because of us, but because they notice. Seeing the power of story and representation for my own child and his cousins, however, has only affirmed the importance of the work I do on E/D/I.

Children begin recognizing race at about the age of 3. I'd known this fact on an academic level, but seeing it in my own child reinforced how important teaching anti-bias is. Humans naturally categorize things. It helps to sort and order the world around us. We categorize by all types of things, including race. What cannot be emphasized enough is that children recognize the differences in skin and hair and eyes and noses and mouths. They notice differences in gender and ability. This is true in the books they read, the TV shows and movies they watch, *and* the real world. They notice when things are different, but also when things are the same. In a diverse society, such as the one we live in, we should teach appreciation of the differences, instead of forcing everyone into the same box. Too often, we attach bias to this recognition.

Although the United States has always had a lot of different people from a lot of different cultures, there has long been a drive to show only one. Consequently, this one story has been called "normal" and considered superior to all other stories. The exclusion of identities, especially identities that were not seen as a part of mainstream American culture, was especially true for young children. When kids see representation or, conversely, lack of representation, it helps shape the way they see the world. It molds the narrative of what is possible. Much of the public, and the public library, is waking up to the fact that representation has been pretty limited. It has taken social media (e.g., We Need Diverse Books, and Marley Dias's #1000BlackGirlBooks) to unveil how the publishing industry has abetted erasure in children's literature. For too long, children have been shown only a single story in school, in books, and on TV. By not focusing on diversity, by being part of and primarily associating with the dominant culture, librarians can quite easily select materials with limited representation.

This is how bias prospers. A lot of times librarians do not realize that the books they choose consistently emphasize a single way of life. This focus can be unintentional, but it reflects a superiority that is rooted in white supremacy. Such librarians think that representation of other identities makes the quality "lesser than." In order to begin the work of including all identities in our storytimes, we first have to do some self-work. In our modern era, the words *racist* or *racism* bring to mind very visual images of burning crosses, lynchings, or the beatings and dog attacks seen in documentaries. That's overt racism. Implicit biases, on the other hand, are thought processes that are often unconscious but that hold negative judgments about race or about a certain type of representation. To stop radicalization toward explicit racism, we must develop tools to begin disrupting implicit biases at an early age. Not changing the narrative is harmful. In order to start, we must have some understanding of the history and policies and laws that have shaped racial exclusion.

The American Academy of Pediatrics has a policy statement about the impact of racism on child and adolescent health: "Children can distinguish the phenotypic differences associated with race during infancy; therefore, effective management of difference as normative is important in a diverse society."[2] In a recent study of intersectional biases, researchers found that "preschool-aged children's implicit and explicit evaluations of Black boys were less positive than their evaluations of Black girls, white boys, or white girls."[3] Early childhood educators have spent more than thirty years putting together an anti-bias curriculum to help provide tools to disrupt biases. In 1991 the Southern Poverty Law Center created Teaching Tolerance, which was one of the earliest resources for promoting anti-bias practices with young children. (In 2021 Teaching Tolerance was renamed Learning for Justice.)

Children's perceptions about race were first launched into national attention when the NAACP asked two psychologists, Kenneth and Mamie Clark, to study the effects of segregation on Black children.

The NAACP needed help to provide evidence in the *Brown v. Board of Education* (347 U.S. 483) case. Chief Justice Earl Warren commented that this social science study was groundbreaking in showing the harmful effects of segregation. Although this study was not perfect, it paved the way for better research about implicit biases.

American policy is shaped to give some people more than others, which makes some people think that they are inherently "superior" to others. For example, the 1896 *Plessy v. Ferguson* (163 U.S. 537) decision introduced the separate but equal doctrine that supported Jim Crow laws. Unfortunately, everything was separate and nothing was equal. The NAACP took cases for more "than six decades to show that states failed to provide anything approximating as equal for black citizens."[4] In *Missouri ex rel. Gaines v. Canada* (305 U.S. 337 (1938)), "Missouri defined equal as paying for black people to get their legal education in Nebraska or Iowa."[5] In the United States, the laws have set things up to be unequal. This inequality was set up racially, whereby the majority—people of European descent—were allowed to take part in the economy, laws, and policy and the minority were not. Legally, public education has not been desegregated for more than one lifetime. Even as we are getting more diverse as a society, geographically, we are more segregated than ever.

Libraries Can Contribute to Change

I was attracted to anti-bias early childhood education teaching because it is about making life better for *all* children. White children are not the only ones who live in the world, and *all* children have a place in it. Self-worth is important as kids grow up, and if they actively see themselves devalued, erased, or not contributing to a larger narrative of positive achievement, then they are taking in the message that there is something wrong with them.

We can change this message. Human differences are something to celebrate. We, as librarians, get the opportunity to present differences in a positive, celebratory manner. When people walk into the library space, they have access to so much quality information and so many experiences. Libraries are in a unique position to help people learn how to do community building. In the book *Anti-Bias Education for Young*

Children and Ourselves, the authors write, "It is important to remember that it is not human differences that undermine children's development but unfair hurtful treatment based upon these differences."[6] To deny this truth or to pretend you don't see race and diversity (color blindness) is to lie to yourself. It becomes problematic when one race is said to be normal, "right," or superior to others. When this one race has power to set up systems and policy and government, members of that race can easily shape those structures for their own benefit. In a *Washington Post* interview, Ibram X. Kendi, the author of *Stamped from the Beginning*, speaks to this problem: "'Fooled by racist ideas,' he admits, 'I did not fully realize that the only thing wrong with Black people is that we think there is something wrong with Back people.'"[7]

I wrote *Let's Talk About Race in Storytimes* and chose to focus on the identity of race (Black) and the ethnic identity of African American.

As I began thinking about how I could apply anti-bias practices to storytimes, I first started studying how early childhood education practices incorporate anti-bias education. A lot of E/D/I is generalized in order to reach a broad audience. Libraries spend a lot of time sending employees to generalized training that may cover certain aspects to take into their professional work. As I started my research, I noticed that not a lot of early childhood education pertained to the library space.

The library and our storytimes can be the perfect space for this education. When I was in library school, I interned at Monroe County Public Library in Bloomington, Indiana. One of the early literacy librarians was a singer. She knew the importance of music education and blended it into her storytimes. Having an undergraduate degree in music education, I loved that she was able to blend her passions so effortlessly. I remembered thinking that the early literacy space could be used to blend teaching the foundation of literacy with teaching social and emotional "literacy skills." When I started down the path of making anti-bias work an official part of my library work, I started looking at other industries that have been doing this work for years.

There is no blueprint for adding anti-bias practices into the storytime space. But there needs to be. Children see and identify race, and if we can teach them how to do this well, society will be better off. The point of anti-bias training is that all children should feel proud of who they are without needing to be superior. In order to do that, children need tools. They need proper language to show respect not only for themselves but also for others. Early childhood education is about fostering that personal identity, whereas anti-bias education is about nurturing the social identity. As the authors of the article "Understanding Anti-Bias Education" state, "Social identities include (but are not limited to) gender, racial, ethnic, cultural, religious, and economic class groups."[8]

As librarians, it is important that we use our storytime spaces to model to caregivers how to foster positive social identity. Because of advances in technology, social media platforms have allowed children an earlier exposure to people who are different from them. Often, children are unsure about how to navigate their responses. Think of all the viral videos of kids saying derogatory words or being explicitly racist and the consequences that may have followed. Even in our most recent presidential election, candidates were arguing about the effectiveness of integrated schools and busing, as you can hear in podcasts such as *The Problem We All Live With* or *Nice White Parents*.

Libraries are needed more than ever to help facilitate conversation and dialogues for the public who may not have community center infrastructure or religious institutions that inspire trust. Harnessing the public trust to create a culture rooted in helping all children become their full selves with an appreciation of respect for all people is needed now more than ever. Librarianship has power. You can provide credible information backed by science and not ignorance. You can help build empathy for and understanding of cultural differences through *so many books*. Most importantly, you can challenge stereotypes and provide positive representation.

BOOKS + TALKING POINTS

I Am Every Good Thing
BY DERRICK BARNES, ILLUSTRATED BY GORDON C. JAMES
"I am not what they call me" is a great way to talk about how society may refer to certain communities in a bad way. Those names should not have any power on the self-esteem of a young Black child.

Whose Knees Are These?
BY JABARI ASIM, ILLUSTRATED BY LEUYEN PHAM

You can use this book to point out the universal simi-
larities that make us human. The important part is to
not ignore the skin tone. You might say, "Look at the
baby's brown knees! Point to your baby's knees! We may look different
on the outside—and that is okay!—but our hearts are all beating the
same language of love."

A Place Inside of Me: A Poem to Heal the Heart
BY ZETTA ELLIOTT, ILLUSTRATED BY NOA DENMON

Share this book with caregivers to help them explain
#BlackLivesMatter or #StopAsianHate. Here is a script
that you can use with this book: "Share with your child
your feelings about race when reading picture books.
Naming your feelings will help your child identify
their feelings and emotions when race comes up in their daily lives,
at school, in social media, or in their local community. You could start
by asking, 'What have you heard?' When they tell you, you might
follow up by saying, 'It makes me so sad when I hear about bad things
happening to people of color. Yet when I see our community coming
together to say that it's not okay, I feel proud to belong here.'"

What's the Difference? Being Different Is Amazing
BY DOYIN RICHARDS

This is a wonderful story filled with kids who all look
different. It encourages listening to people's stories
and rejecting color blindness.

I Am Brown
BY ASHOK BANKER, ILLUSTRATED BY SANDHYA PRABHAT

Use this book to highlight cultural differences. You
might say, "Did you know that it's okay to point out
cultural differences when reading picture books? When
exploring those differences with your child, reinforce
that *different* and *weird* are not the same thing. Isn't it great that there
are so many people who do different things?" (For educators, this is a
great book to remind us that identities are not just filled with struggle.

Identities are multifaceted and provide a global view. Do not forget to bring joy and happiness into your storytime space!)

Black Is a Rainbow Color
BY ANGELA JOY, ILLUSTRATED BY EKUA HOLMES
This is a wonderful story to remind us that black is not just a color . . . it is also a culture. The author provides educational material to adapt at any level.

---

o o o SELF-REFLECTION o o o

> On a scale of 1 to 5, how comfortable are you with talking about race?

> In thinking about *Let's Talk About Race in Storytimes*, why does this work matter to you?

> If you are not comfortable with talking about race, what practices can help you become more comfortable?

> What will you do if you make a mistake or if someone calls you out for making an assumption or showing an implicit bias?

> What social justice terms do you know? How would these terms help build shared language among storytime practitioners?

NOTES

1. German Lopez, "The Sneaky Language Today's Politicians Use to Get Away with Racism and Sexism," *Vox*, February 1, 2016, https://www.vox.com/2016/2/1/10889138/coded-language-thug-bossy.
2. M. Trent, D. G. Dooley, J. Dougé, Section on Adolescent Health, Council on Community Pediatrics and Committee on Adolescence, "The Impact of Racism on Child and Adolescent Health," *Pediatrics* 144, no. 2 (August 2019): e20191765, https://doi.org/10.1542/peds.2019-1765.

3. D. R. Perszyk, R. F. Lei, G. V. Bodenhausen, J. A. Richeson, and S. R. Waxman, "Bias at the Intersection of Race and Gender: Evidence from Preschool-Aged Children," *Developmental Science* (2019): 22e12788, https://doi.org/10.1111/desc.12788.

4. Carol Anderson, with Tonya Bolden, *We Are Not Yet Equal: Understanding Our Racial Divide* (New York: Bloomsbury, 2018).

5. Anderson, *We Are Not Yet Equal.*

6. L. Derman-Sparks and J. O. Edwards, with C. M. Goins, *Anti-Bias Education for Young Children and Ourselves*, 2nd ed. (Washington, DC: National Association for the Education of Young Children, 2020).

7. Carlos Lozada, "The Racism of Good Intentions," *Washington Post*, April 15, 2016, https://www.washingtonpost.com/news/book-party/ wp/2016/04/15/the-racism-of-good-intentions/.

8. Louise Derman-Sparks and Julie Olsen Edwards, "Understanding Anti-Bias Education: Bringing the Four Core Goals to Every Facet of Your Curriculum," *Young Children* 74, no. 5 (November 2019), https://www.naeyc.org/resources/pubs/yc/nov2019/understanding -anti-bias.

THEY SEE YOU

Whenever I did readers' advisory at the public service desk, I always included authors of color in my book recommendation lineup, whether for sports, comics, or whatever the child was interested in. I always paid attention to how caregivers responded when I showed them my recommendations after they asked for a book selection. Parents of color would get really excited if I was able to find a book representation that matched the skin tone of the child. I remember giving a woman a book on Black mermaids and though her daughter looked confused, the mom burst into an accolade, saying she could not wait to read it because she always wanted to see Black mermaids when she was a child. Small interactions like this have always stuck with me.

At its core, *Let's Talk About Race in Storytimes* is about realizing how the "dominant culture" influences the storytime space and providing tools to help disrupt biases and promote healthy dialogue about race and diversity.

When our local museum, the Grand Rapids Art Museum, had a David Wiesner exhibit, I was asked to train docents about the topic "The Importance of Storytelling in Art." I focused on the science behind the creation of picture books and how important wordless picture books are to building early literacy skills. In a study of wordless picture books, the researchers noted that "for centuries people have conveyed meaning through the use of visual images, without the aid of written text."[1] As library workers, we know that reading to a child helps in so many ways—the cadence of language, varied sentence structure, the rhythm of the language—but books also do a great job of giving opportunities to observe the world. Children notice a lot more than we realize. And they are just inherently curious. In early childhood development, we know that kids gravitate to pictures as they develop their language skills. As kids enter different phases (baby to toddler to preschooler), they can begin layering their developmental skills (understanding words and pictures) to blend in a natural rhythm. They see stark and bold contrast of colors. As their development progresses, they start categorizing skin tone colors. By the age of 6 to 8, kids can sort others into racial groups.[2] They see who is there, and who is missing. Without an understanding of history, laws, and policies, children can be susceptible to biased ideas very early. They want to understand how the world works and are often trying to process the world around them through thoughts and questions.

As the saying goes, "a picture is worth a thousand words." When it comes to representation via pictures, those words can change the scope of what is possible. There have been so many missed opportunities in children's literature to help foster a child's imagination about the positives of social identities outside the dominant culture.

For too long in the United States, the dominant story (representation—defined here as schoolbooks, television hosts, movie stars, models/actors, news anchors, bosses, people who hold "good" jobs, stable families, politicians) has centered white people, most often men. Seeing this representation over and over, in place after place, subtly tells children that *only* white men can hold those jobs. So they associate power with that representation. This image creates what has been called a "single story."

The Danger of a Single Story

The writer Chimamanda Adichie speaks about this aspect in her TED talk titled "The Danger of a Single Story."[3] When she was a child, she loved writing stories and did so quite often. All the books she was exposed to had girls with golden hair, eating apples. In the world around her, there was neither gold hair nor apples. There was tightly curled hair and mangos. Because the stories that she read had only characters with golden hair eating apples, she thought *all* stories had to have these components. This perception was limiting. When she got a little older and found her own voice, she was able to change this belief, and she began writing stories from her perspective about the world as she saw it. This approach opened her writing, enriching literature.

The "danger" Adichie is referring to is that she, and girls like her, thought they could only tell one type of story if they wanted to write books. She had talent as a writer, but was forced to create content that wasn't familiar to her. Once she realized that she could craft narratives about the world around her in the way she saw and experienced that world, from her point of view, she was able to get out of the trap of a single story and find her own voice. How many people are there, like her, out there, who could have done likewise but weren't so inventive? Or got "writer's block" because they could not imagine the context?

Adichie encourages listeners to expand representation so that children are exposed to stories and characters of all different types. If we're not intentional in showing the beauty and diversity of the world, we can fall into the trap of telling one story—a single story.

The problem with a single story is that children are subtly *told* that this is how things work. And if this is how things work, you must assimilate and be like those people in order to get and hold those positions. This requirement applies to how you act, how you dress, and what you value. This single story becomes the starting point. And this is how implicit bias begins.

Identity Is Important

In order to build empathy, you have to listen to experiences outside your own. Often adults do not know how to manage self-awareness and social awareness, especially when that awareness relates to cultural nuances. This experience can be fun for a child, but adults have to be able to separate their own trauma related to differences and policies from any harm that might come from that trauma. Frequently, it is during school that oppression really resonates in kids who are developing social identities. (See the text box "Know Your Terms" to further define identity.) Usually this experience of oppression is due to the misunderstanding, and often the misinterpreted teachings, of history. This cultural dominance is an offshoot of the ways in which history is taught in schools. The narrative is not about a shared history of all Americans; rather, BIPOC contributions to history are seen as inferior to, or a side note of, white achievements. BIPOC kids have a tendency to meet themselves during shameful moments in history whereas white kids are seen as achievers and contributors throughout *all* of history.

When we show only these stories, we are unintentionally reinforcing biases and not necessarily helping children get ready to participate in a society that is asking for tolerance and acceptance of differences. If we can remove the stigma attached to skin color and hair and empower kids to respectfully connect with each other without ostracizing anyone because of their differences, think of how much better our society would be. If we can help share more than a single story, it may go a long way when the next generation of doctors, civil servants, and private citizens grows up.

The implicit bias is created because mainstream media have shown only that single story. A lot of work for E/D/I, and training therein—this book included—is an attempt to show and celebrate the beautiful range of diversity that is the world. In the real world, as it is rather than how it's portrayed through history books, many things are "normal." When we show children in our storytimes the range of people in the world, it helps them learn that they can do and be anything. It shows that "normal" isn't the dominant culture but, rather, whatever they'd like to do or be.

When children ask questions, there is often an inherent fear or "taboo" associated with answering. Giving caregivers appropriate tools and support may help them feel empowered and ready to answer those questions. Additionally, it will help encourage honesty when they do not have answers. My hope is that if we can tackle the subject of race, then all identities can be talked about in a healthy and celebrated manner. Rather than judge what children see as good or bad, we should be aware that *how* we show these things can either liberate or oppress. We can showcase the diverse world or continue to spread the false narrative of a single story. Children can create a narrative that is biased or open, depending on how we show the stories.

KNOW YOUR TERMS

What Is Identity?

According to Learning for Justice, *identity* has two definitions:

- The collective aspect of the set of characteristics by which a thing or person is definitively recognized or known
- The set of behavioral or personal characteristics by which an individual is recognizable as a member of a group

There are different ways to break down identity. It can be visible or invisible and also personal or social. Ultimately you will have to map out your identity and see how that relates to our larger society. When you have an understanding of your own identity, you can start thinking about how other people's identities are similar or different.

What Is Power?

"Power is having influence, authority, or control over people and/or resources."[a]

In the storytime space, you have control over the people and the resources in that room. No matter your institution's budget, you or your storytime team decides what those resources look like.

What Is Oppression?

"Oppression is the combination of prejudice and institutional power which creates a system that discriminates against some groups (often called 'target groups') and benefits other groups (often called 'dominant groups')."[b]

How Does Identity Relate to Power and Its Counterpart, Oppression?

In order to understand our caregivers' identities or identities that may be missing from the storytime space, we have to first unpack our own identity. If we understand all the layers of how our identity relates to power and oppression, we can then think about what power looks like in a storytime space. If we have a base level of understanding through our identities and power, we can use the storytime space as a place to oppress or liberate.

[a] Katie Dover-Taylor, Jody Gray, and Amita Lonial, "Understanding Power, Identity, and Oppression," webinar, December 5, 2017, https://www.ala.org/pla/sites/ala.org.pla/files/content/onlinelearning/webinars/Understanding-Power-Identity-and-Oppression-Webinar-Handout.pdf

[b] Dover-Taylor, Gray, and Lonial, "Understanding Power."

Representation Matters

When I was young, my mom sat me down and told me I'd mainly see African Americans shown through a negative lens on television and in the newspaper. She made sure to tell me that this portrayal was used to instill fear. Such sensationalism sold the papers and advertisements. People bought newspapers with the scary headlines or would sit through the commercials to hear the "scary" story. She never wanted me to be ashamed of my skin because of how the media chose to represent blackness. She was explaining to my young mind that the main way I'd see African Americans was a singular, negative way, although we have all types of experiences. She knew that there would be overrepresentation of "negatives" regarding blackness. My mother knew, and reinforced to me, that African Americans—like all people from all races—have vastly different experiences and come in all shapes, sizes, colors, and abilities. Much of the Black history that is taught in schools is about African Americans who were able to break into the mainstream, overlooking countless other stories of Black excellence. This is why my parents made such a point of taking my brother and me to museums and other places that showcased Black excellence.

My mother made sure that we read about the enslaved seamstress Elizabeth Keckley, who bought her freedom and sewed dresses for Abraham Lincoln's wife. There was Ida B. Wells, who visited the South to investigate and shed light on the injustices of lynchings by Southern white mobs. My mother also made sure that we saw the full range of the Black experience. We visited museums that showed Black excellence, but to balance this out, we volunteered at the Mission and nursing homes. My parents made sure we could see extreme poverty, so that we knew how good we had it.

In the past, children's books were not favorable to BIPOC. *Uncle Tom's Cabin* by Harriet Beecher Stowe first introduced the pickaninny caricature to the world. *Little Black Sambo* was highly popular during the 1930s and '40s, exploiting this "pickaninny style," and even in early films Black children were portrayed this way. Famous children's librarians, including Charlemae Hill Rollins, Pura Belpré, and Augusta

Braxton Baker, laid frameworks for evaluating children's books that still hold true. When I was growing up, representation (in older movies) of African Americans was limited to the role of maid or servant. They were the ones who shined the shoes, served the food, and lived in the "bad neighborhood." They were under arrest, anti-law, and often shown as poor. One or two successful characters were praised as standing out from their peers and rising above their situation, but this was celebrated as being *atypical* rather than the norm. Even in the popular books, the people of color were pleasing to white America. They were characters who had assimilated, had beaten great odds, or fit into the Magical Negro camp. This assimilation narrative is perpetuated when children enter a storytime space and never see a book portraying just the Black experience. Diversity often is showcased in one book covering *all* identities instead of focusing on a single identity of BIPOC families. Furthermore, diversity coverage of Black identity is frequently rooted only in the heaviness of oppression and never in the resilience of resistance or all the little, joyous moments that make up our identity. When the stories do show minority representation, these books featuring BIPOC are often presented only during heritage or cultural month storytimes.

What my mother conveyed to me is a common experience for BIPOC. We are often presented in a singular way. The sheer number of movies and books and shows and stories of white people naturally shows the range of the mainstream experience. In school, kids read about Irish, Polish, German, Italian, and British history. British literature is even a required high school course. This variety, however, doesn't extend to the other cultures that make up America.

Teaching children how to properly respect other cultures—especially when those cultures may be tied to a history rooted in shame—can seem difficult. Most of our American history has not been taught properly in its full and complicated context. Our communities can seem insular regarding networks and resources. Librarians can help build bridges to these other experiences that affirm to all children that they are deserving of respect or that they should practice empathy when listening to a story that may treat groups unfairly.

Erasure

As librarians, we wonder why different parts of our communities are missing from representation and then we learn that there were laws and policies that *excluded* races. Academics have coined a term for this lack of representation—*erasure*. In a *New York Times Magazine* article, Parul Sehgal stated,

> To engage with the lives of others, white audiences would have to encounter something far more frightening: their irrelevance. They would have to reckon with the fact that the work will not always speak to them, orient them, flatter them with tales of their munificence or infamy, or comfort them with stereotypes. If there is an opposite of erasure, it is allowing for full personhood in all its idiosyncrasies.[4]

Erasure perpetuates a cycle that causes missed interactions by "equalizing" life experiences. Although humanity has universal threads like birth and death, other cultural differences, whether physical or historical, are okay.

This same type of definition changing goes for books and really adds importance to how you model what the library looks like. Does storytime create a space where kids can see themselves outside heritage months? How are different identities handled when presented in a book? If kids are exposed to just one thing, or one type of story, that becomes their normal. This is how bias is created. Libraries often talk about low literacy rates (often just for minorities) or the fact that we are seeing only one type of family in our storytimes (often white), yet we do not take the time to ask questions about what caregivers are experiencing in our space. About why we are seeing only one type of person. Are caregivers seeing enough representation of themselves? Do they feel valued?

Appreciating Difference

As storytime instructors, we can be the ones to nurture appreciation of differences within diverse individuals. When kids enter our library space, they will see all types of library users. It is important to create a

LET'S TALK ABOUT RACE IN STORYTIMES SCRIPTS

Storytime Introduction

"My name is [insert name here] and I am [insert position here] at the [insert library name].

Did you know that staff are here to help you match up perfect books to your child? Whether your child is a baby, a toddler, or preschool age, it is never too early for encouraging reading. Here at the library, we want to help children become comfortable working, living, and communing alongside people who look different from themselves."

Introducing an Author of Color

"Discover a whole range of authors in our picture book section!!"

"[Jerry Pinkney] is an award-winning [African American] illustrator and author who has written some *amazing* picture books! Let's read this one together. If you ever need any help finding different authors of color, please let us know! We would love to show you books representing [African American artists]."

Note on Racial Terminology

Please do research before assigning cultural or ethnic identity to skin tone colors. If the book or author does not assign or explicitly state an ethnicity, then take one from the Cooper Hewitt Guidelines for Image Description (https://www.cooperhewitt.org/cooper-hewitt-guidelines-for-image-description/):

> When describing the skin tone of a person use non-ethnic terms such as "light-skinned" or "dark-skinned" when clearly visible. Because of its widespread use, we recommend the emoji terms for skin tone as follows: Light Skin Tone, Medium-Light Skin Tone, Medium Skin Tone, Medium-Dark Skin Tone, Dark Skin Tone. Also, where skin tone is obvious, one can use more specific terms such as *black* and *white*, or where known and verified, ethnic identity can be included with the visual information: Asian, African, Latinx/o/a.

If the book explicitly states an identity, then it is okay to say the race or ethnicity and add the word *American* (African American, Muslim American, Asian American, Arab American). These terms could go out of date, or groups of people may choose to be identified differently, so it is important to be aware and do research to make sure you are using appropriate terms. You can also use the generalized terms *POC* (people of color) or *BIPOC* (Black, Indigenous, and people of color).

space where kids of all identities feel safe and welcomed. The library can be the place where children see all types of people in all types of settings. Unless we are exposed to all types of people, we will never be able to build the social and emotional intelligence needed to create a better society. Empathy is a process, not a product. We librarians can be the ones, through our storytimes, to show the vast array of humanity, normalizing all people and talking positively about difference. Librarians have the power to make different people or experiences either visible or invisible in the storytime space. Check out the text box *"Let's Talk About Race in Storytimes* Scripts" to help you practice making everyone feel that they are seen and belong in your space.

Bias and Identity

In order to talk about race in a healthy, productive way, you need to talk about bias and identity. In her essay "Five Faces of Oppression," Iris Young writes about cultural dominance, the concept of showing that one culture and one way of being is right. In a cultural landscape where not challenging the norm is valued, these biases continue. In storytimes, when we only present narratives of children who have two parents that are the same (usually white), a house, a car, and other such "innocent" elements, children internalize that this image of life is the norm and that anything that is not presented, talked about, or discussed is "other." A lot of the time, "other" is not seen as "good" or "belonging"; rather, it is "abnormal." When this portrayal is normalized, it creates a stereotype that children have to *un*-learn later. If we add all types of stories to storytime, especially for young children, and show examples of a diverse way of seeing and doing things, then we are doing our part to create a better, more open society.

I first started testing *Let's Talk About Race in Storytimes* in my own community, as a part of booktalks. *Let's Talk About Race in Storytimes* was initially created for children ages 0 to 5 to help with social and emotional intelligence formation. I went throughout the community, showing different books to kids. I would then give booktalks to children, mentioning racial differences in the books and affirming that it was okay if the children pointed out those differences. Caregivers didn't know how to respond. (Often, caregivers needed help in understanding that we were there to help match books to their child.) Some caregivers would come up to me afterward and ask if pointing out the differences was okay. Others would ask if they were racist if they ignored the differences or pretended that their child didn't point out a difference. I realized that caregivers were really unequipped to talk about race, especially in a way that was knowledgeable and affirming. I call it the *circular osmosis effect*. We think that children will learn about differences through other places in the community (school, caregivers, other diverse settings), and we leave children to figure it out on their own, usually to their own detriment. This is why we need to actively discuss differences.

So I made a tool kit. The first thing I did was give children *permission* to talk about race. I'd say some version of "It's okay to point out the difference in people. It's beautiful." Letting caregivers know that it is okay—and natural—if kids notice differences is a good first step. The second step was finding out how I could encourage caregivers to "check in" with their child as the child begins processing identities around them and to give the child the respectful tools to do that.

Sometimes, when people notice injustice or notice problems that need to be fixed, they do not take action because of just how daunting the problem is. If a problem is huge, systemic, and long-standing, mounting a defense can be taxing. It is hard to know what to do, and one response is to do nothing. But doing nothing just makes the problem continue. This is what I found so empowering about Black Lives Matter's suggestion to stay in our lane and help there. For me, my lane is the library, and when I read about Black Lives Matter, I decided that I needed to take action in my field. As institutions funded by and existing for the public, libraries can be the places to have these types of conversations and normalize them. By doing so, we are accomplishing two things: one, we're modeling to caregivers *how* they too can have conversations about diversity, and two, we can show how to *normalize* conversations about difference and representation.

I started engaging in this work in very different ways. When doing readers' advisory, I was very cognizant of recommending books not just by white authors. That awareness led me to being vocal about making sure that parents understood that our picture book collection included *all* kinds of books. When I was a storytime instructor, it was important for me to uplift all representations of my community and make everyone feel a sense of belonging when they stepped inside the storytime space. Some people fear this approach or think it sounds boring, but rest assured—we had fun. Learning about identities does not mean that we have to spend time only discussing oppression in those identities. We should look for joy!

As the manager of the library, I made sure to put options on our displays for authors of all races. One approach was to create a Books by the Stack display that had all different genres of books by all different types of authors. If I wanted to exhibit an Indigenous experience, there was Cynthia Smith's *Jingle Dancer* or James and Joseph Bruchac's *Rabbit's Snow Dance*. If we wanted to showcase the Black experience, then Floyd Cooper's *Max and the Tag-Along Moon* or Connie Schofield-Morrison's *I Got the Rhythm* were my go-to books.

For baby storytimes I would showcase books like *Whose Knees Are These?* by Jabari Asim. After storytimes, I would guide conversations organically, letting caregivers know that if they wanted award-winning reads, there are many awards (other than the Caldecott) that celebrate diverse books and provide a sense of identity outside whiteness (e.g., the Coretta Scott King Book Award, the Pura Belpré Award, and the Asian/Pacific American Award for Literature). These types of lists and awards are great places to start because they are already vetted. Selecting books from lists like these provides a way to balance a child's interest and to let parents know that there are different lived experiences in picture books, which is okay.

The final step in being able to talk about race productively is to confront our own bias. The foundation of this work rests on unpacking your own identity so that you know who you are and can always be conscious of others and their identities and lived experiences. Understanding our identities in relation to the dominant culture is instrumental in being able to bring our best selves and different experiences to our communities, whether homogeneous or mixed race. I will touch on this topic only lightly because there are copious numbers of books and education facilitators that do a better job of detailing how this understanding affects us. Two terms to keep in mind are *microaggression* and *micro-inequity*, which can result in talking about race improperly.[5] According to *Merriam-Webster*, a microaggression is "a comment or action that subtly and often unconsciously or unintentionally expresses a prejudiced attitude toward a member of a marginalized group" (https://www.merriam-webster.com/dictionary/microaggression).

A micro-inequity is specific to the workplace environment and potentially affects performance and damages self-esteem. Whereas microaggressions usually arise in conversation, micro-inequities can take a variety of forms, including a gesture, a specific treatment, or even a tone of voice. Many times, micro-inequities are passive and unconscious.

It's good to be aware of these events in a storytime space. Microaggressions are easily spotted in a storytime setting. They show up in many ways, like assuming that people are foreign-born because of how they look and asking, "Where are you from?" Or in pathologizing cultural values and communication styles: "Why are Black people so loud?" Or in comments that are unintentionally offensive, such as "When I look at you, I don't see color." A guide sheet outlining microaggressions is usually enough to encourage thinking about past or present conversations or comments that are offensive.

Micro-inequities affect our library space. If you recognize your identities and the fact that you hold power in the storytime space, you can then start to unpack certain inequities that you may not even know you are committing. Are you aware of how different cultures use space? We are aware of how children use space, but often we do not allow caregivers to be their full, authentic selves in the library space. Are you consistently mispronouncing your storytime attendees' names? Have you given up learning them? Are you consistently overrepresenting a culture because it is easier than showcasing one that is outside your lived experience? We often do not take into account that how we interact with space will be different. Some cultures will JUST BE LOUD.

In my teaching I use the example of Black teens walking into the library space. People often will react negatively. Their body may tense up, or they look frequently in the teens' direction. They may give nonverbal cues, such as being afraid or nervous, sighing, raising their voice, or even rolling their eyes, before the teens have cleared the area. Micro-inequities reflect our lack of recognition that cultures share space differently.

Librarians have to be understanding of their space. When I was a branch manager, two Black women who hadn't seen each other in a long time were at the computer excitedly catching up. A white patron got mad and wanted to make a complaint about how loud they were. When I told him they hadn't seen each other in a long time and were just catching up (the same way I had always seen my mom catching up with her family), he lodged a complaint about me, saying I was "one of these people and wouldn't let these other people be quiet."

Such micro-inequities reflect how we feel about other cultures and about differences in ways of functioning, including the use of space. "Space" can have many meanings, including barriers to accessing storytimes, and not just the immediate "creating a storytime space with floor circles." I am talking about everything that goes into getting everyone into the "storytime space," including marketing and promotion. And though you can control some things and not others, depending on your organization, it is helpful to realize that your whole community may not be represented in storytime. Because of a lack of trust, some community members may feel that entering the library is not for them. Is there a way you can bridge this mistrust? The ways in which different cultures use space in their efforts to build community will be different. If you are out in community spaces that are different from those of the dominant culture, you can start to glean understanding that can help you create a more inclusive library storytime space.

In order to talk about race in storytime, and to have representation of all people, you must be intentional. Intentionality is essential because the counter has been true as well. The single-story, erasure, and melting pot concepts are also intentional. Jim Crow laws were intentional. Segregated schools were intentional. Lynchings and Muslim bans were intentional. There's a certain kind of person who equates diversity and representation with being "liberal" or with trying to change the country, while overlooking the intentionality of our history. When people say such things, they're essentially trying to push a single story and erasure.

When you're not intentional, you can accidentally, unintentionally, tell the single story. There are different levels of entry to this work. If you think of E/D/I work as a big, endless pool, the first step is to dip your toe in the water—for example, by making sure to showcase different stories when you set up your storytime room. From there, wade into the water by explaining to parents all the different types of awards created to honor excellence in these different lived experiences of picture books. Wade farther in by making sure you are researching authors and how they identify in order to portray them and their work respectfully. Next, you can start swimming by empowering caregivers so that kids will notice the difference and have thoughtful, meaningful conversations. Swim faster by building language and engaging in empathy. This may be hard for people new to E/D/I work. At the beginning E/D/I does take work and intention. It can bring up fears and doubts and difficult conversations. Many times, the word *professional* is synonymous with *expert*. Experts do not like to look vulnerable or have their expertise questioned. E/D/I work in storytime will bring out vulnerabilities and create a space for failure. In doing so, it is with the hope that one will embrace learning from one's mistakes. So, let's look at the nuts and bolts of overcoming our fears, talking about race and storytime, and talking to our colleagues.

What some people find uncomfortable is figuring out how to model differences appropriately when it comes to topics like race. This dilemma is especially true if the one attempting to model E/D/I is a part of the racial majority.

The answer depends on the space and the developmental needs of the child. Having caregivers talk to a child at length about race could be time-consuming in a chaotic storytime environment. However, caregivers can bring one-on-one attention and real-world connections in discussing a book.

Sometimes, because we feel awkward about talking about race, we overcompensate. Usually, overcompensation can result in microaggressions or interrupting, indications of a lack of respect for caregivers or their culture. Centering your talk on a parent tip can help mitigate a sense of failure in talking about race. The final stage of a parent tip is the affirmation. Remember that affirmations are about the celebration of difference. It is not enough to just "acknowledge" or "point out" the difference; follow up by reminding everyone that it is great to have these differences. That follow-up is called an "affirmation."

Tips to Share with Parents

- **While reading to your child, it is okay to point out racial differences.** "Is that skin lighter or darker than your own? Did you know that we can be born with different skin tone colors? Well, this skin tone is called _____."
- **Point out cultural differences.** When exploring differences, reinforce that "different" and "weird" are not the same thing. "Why is her hair weird?" "Her hair type is different. People can have straight, curly, or wavy hair. I think it is great that we are all different."
- **Share feelings about race.** Share with your child your feelings about race when reading picture books. "It makes me mad that certain groups of people like African Americans were treated differently."
- **Use the words *unfair* and *fair* when talking about racial stereotypes in picture books.** "Wow, this picture book only included white, male inventors. That's unfair. Did you know that _____ created things too? Let's read about some famous _____ inventors."
- **Respect their observations.** Respect your child's curiosity about the world around them by answering their hard and sometimes embarrassing observations. "Let me think about that for a while" or "That is a good question" or "I do not know" are great starting responses.

Affirmations

Affirmations are very important in order not to marginalize or "other" differences in kids. Affirmations are at the very core of celebrating differences. Here is a list of some affirmations that you can use during storytimes.

Storytime Affirmations

- "Aren't our differences extraordinary?"
- "We may look different on the outside (and that is okay!), but our hearts are all beating the same language of love."

Physical Affirmations

Sometimes kids are curious and point out differences. That's okay! You can let them know that a lot of physical differences are scientific.

- "This is legit science [for hair, skin, genetics]!"
- "Look at this character's skin! Is their skin lighter than your own? Darker than your own? Did you know we are all born with different skin tone colors? Isn't that *amazing*?"
- "Hey, everyone, touch your hair! Do you all see this character's hair? Did you know that we are born with different hair textures? Some hair is curly, some hair is wavy, some hair is straight. Curls can be loose or tight. We should celebrate that. Give yourself a hug [model hugging]."
- "What beautiful skin tones! How are they different? Isn't it cool that humans are so similar yet have distinct, wonderful differences?"
- "As you grow up, you will meet people who look like you and others who don't. That's okay! Celebrate that wonder. Listen to their stories."
- "Where are your eyes? Did you know that just like our bodies, our eyes may differ in shape (just ask makeup artists!)? Isn't it terrific that we can all still see all the bright wonders together?"

On Sharing Affirmations

- "People make judgments (or say mean things) when they are afraid of something or don't understand something—like in this story [insert problem here]. That makes me sad. How does it make you feel? What would you do [solution question]?"
- "History has not been kind to people who are different. Laws were created regarding people being different. That makes me angry! It's okay to get mad or frustrated about things sometimes. Show me your mad face!"
- "Everyone feels pain. There is no reason to assume that just because people look different, they cannot experience pain."

Societal/Cultural Affirmations

- Pointing out cultural/societal differences: "Different cultures enjoy different food—like [insert different cultural examples]. You might have even tried some! Remember, because someone eats something that you might not know, it is not weird. It's just different. Being different is okay."
- "Did you know that there are more than six thousand languages? Is that a BIG number or a small number? How can you try to understand someone who doesn't speak the same language as you? How cool that there are so many differences! Someone may not speak in the same language, but humans are *full* of feelings. What are some facial expressions that can express a feeling regardless of 'words'"?
- "Do you remember when you were treated unfairly? [Let the children answer or describe what they think.] Do you think it is okay for people to be treated like this just because they look different? [You might share that laws prohibited some people from being a family, going to school, etc.] Sometimes, families will be different. Some people will not necessarily 'match' physically but are still family! Meeting different people is just an exciting part of being alive!!!!"

Steps to Success

- **Start by affirming racial differences.** "This baby on the cover has brown skin. Look! On this page a baby has a different shade of skin. Our differences are *awesome!*" You can repeat the same thing for toddlers and before the affirmation add: "What shade does it look like?" Give them space to answer and then circle back to how wonderful it is to be human.
- **Add an inclusive picture walk.** A picture walk is the shared activity of previewing the pictures in a storybook.[6] You can use it to model to caregivers how adults and children can interact with pictures before adding on text. A picture walk can help children become familiar with the story before introducing the text. Using the parent tip, *While reading to your child, it is okay to point out*

racial differences, hold up the book while speaking and point out the racial difference. "Is that skin lighter or darker than your own? Did you know that we can be born with different skin tone colors?" Point to the character and ask open-ended questions such as "Do you have dark or light skin? Do I have dark or light skin?" You may choose to add what the skin tone is called. End with an affirmation: "Isn't it great that we are all born with different skin?"

- **Be authentic and intentional.** Encourage parents to talk about race early. "It is okay to point out racial differences in books for all children, from babies to teens. You can talk in more detail about race at different stages, but it is all right to start when they are babies, acknowledging differences in skin, hair, language, or culture."

○○○ SELF-REFLECTION ○○○

▶ Did you grow up talking about race when you were young?

▶ Did you read books about anyone who was from a different culture or ethnicity than your own? What stood out to you?

▶ What is one lesson you learned from a book about a different culture that has an impact on you to this day?

▶ What are some good resources for finding appropriate ethnic and racial terms?

NOTES

1. Marina Mohd Arif and Fatimah Hashim, "Reading from the Wordless: A Case Study on the Use of Wordless Picture Books," *English Language Teaching* 1, no. 1 (2008): 121–26, 10.5539/elt.v1n1p121, https://files.eric.ed.gov/fulltext/EJ1082619.pdf.

2. See Kristin Pauker, Amanda Williams, and Jennifer R. Steele, "Children's Racial Categorization in Context," *Child Development Perspectives* 10, no. 1 (2016): 33–38.

3. Chimamanda Adichie, "The Danger of a Single Story," filmed July 2009, TED video, 18:33, https://www.ted.com/talks/chimamanda _ngozi_adichie_the_danger_of_a_single_story?language=en.

4. Parul Sehgal, "Fighting 'Erasure,'" *The New York Times Magazine*, February 2, 2016, https://www.nytimes.com/2016/02/07/magazine/the-painful-consequences-of-erasure.html.

5. Both terms come from D. W. Sue, C. M. Capodilupo, G. C. Torino, J. M. Bucceri, A. M. B. Holder, K. L. Nadal, and M. Esquilin, "Racial Microaggressions in Everyday Life: Implications for Clinical Practice," *American Psychologist* 62, no. 4 (2007): 271–286, https://doi.org/10.1037/0003-066X.62.4.271.

6. Ellen Milne, "Taking a Picture Walk," *Hands and Voices* (2014), https://www.handsandvoices.org/articles/education/ed/V11-2_picturewalk.htm.

BECOMING A COCONSPIRATOR

T he fact that you're on chapter 3 of this book leads me to believe that you care about bringing about a better world and that you have a desire to do so in a tangible way that helps your community. My hunch is also that a big part of the reason you bought this book is because you question *your* ability to talk about race in a way that is helpful and doesn't add to the problem. You might wonder, "How am I equipped to talk about race?" Or maybe you wonder, "*Can I talk about race?*" The good news is that yes, you can do this! You can overcome that doubt and fear. You are doing the work, and being a champion for diversity and inclusion is the most important part of bringing about a better society. It starts library by library, storytime instructor by storytime instructor.

Before we look at how to overcome fears, I want to be very direct in saying what I'd like you to get out of this chapter; it's so important that I'm going to begin the chapter by saying it directly: *change from being an ally to being a coconspirator.* What does this look like in practical terms? It looks like a wall of moms.

In the summer of 2020, after the killings of Breonna Taylor and George Floyd, there were protests in every state in the country. Few of them got as much attention as those in Portland, Oregon. As the protests were going on, the president brought in the National Guard to fight the people. Protestors fought back. Group after group showed their support of Black Lives Matter in an interesting way. Different groups began standing in front of the Black Lives Matter protests. First, army veterans stood and then, in front of the army vets, stood the Wall of Moms. The Wall of Moms was a group of mothers who said that enough is enough, that *all* people deserve justice and equality, and that if you want to go after this oppressed group that you don't understand, you're first going to have to come through us.

These are coconspirators.

Diversity is a good thing. Diversity provides a richness a monolith cannot. Diversity expands experience. It's something worth fighting for. In my trainings, I tell people that the movement toward a more open and inclusive society needs everyone. There's a popular term— *ally*—which is often used to say you're on the side of the oppressed, and being an ally is a great thing, but it also makes it possible to sit idly by and watch while others do the work of making society more just. And though being an ally is good, being what Alicia Garza calls a *coconspirator* is better. Transitioning your thinking to that of a coconspirator makes you take an active part in making the change.

The change in terminology can be a transformative mental shift. It's a shift from passive to active and is very empowering. Coconspirators *cannot* be silent. I've seen this very personally—even in my own marriage! My husband fit into the category of ally but didn't know what he could do. I'd heard him express frustration about seeing problems but not knowing what to do. I explained the coconspirator thing to him, and it really helped him make sense of the work I am doing. I'll have him explain.

~~~~~~

HI. I'M TOM, JESSICA'S HUSBAND. One thing I did not anticipate when we got married was that being in an interracial marriage would get more difficult as time progressed. I, like a lot of my white friends, thought society was moving forward and things would just keep getting better. The way it was taught to me in school was that things are equal and some people are racist. I learned that there was a Civil Rights Act passed in 1964 and that things have been equal since then. Because laws are equal, all people have the same opportunity. The assumption was that myself, my family, and all white people like us who had immigrated here had worked hard and had earned success.

That's an oversimplification, but my role was to be a good person, care about all people, and that was enough. There'd never been much talk about the system and the effect it had on people.

When I began my professional career, I taught mostly in schools that were impoverished. At these schools, I began waking up to the systemic oppression. I saw how different things were in a community where people did not look like me or have the economic advantages I had. Things I'd taken for granted were luxuries to my students. The assumptions I brought were far from accurate. I tried to help people but didn't really know what to do. Several times when I witnessed injustice, I didn't know how to intercede.

The summer of 2016 changed that. It was the first intimate glimpse of the pain systemic injustice caused my wife. We'd just celebrated one year of marriage. She's typically happy and content in the moment, almost never talks negatively about anyone, and doesn't complain—which is part of what makes her great. She works hard and is a doer. She also takes advantage of downtime more than anyone I'd seen. So it was eye-opening to see the effect that what was happening on the national scene had on her at an individual level. By this time I'd gotten to know a lot of her friends and family much better as well, and saw that this response was not unique to my wife but extended to a lot of people.

You could see or hear on the news just how much the violence against Black bodies was hurting African American people. Seeing the weight and fear and fatigue so close and personal was a game changer for me. She and her friends and family of color echoed the narratives of people of color on television: This happens. We're scared. We're tired. What made it worse, though, was seeing how people reacted. Calling on people to get over it or denying violence against Black bodies is obviously ignorant. Sugarcoating or justifying occasional missteps is also harmful. But what I saw, and why I'm writing this, is that a lot of other reactions—reactions intended to be helpful—also added to the pain and fatigue. Dozens of people reached out to me—family and friends who know I have an African American wife—to ask how she was doing, what they could do, or what was appropriate to ask. I didn't know. (Still don't, really.) But I knew it wasn't asking me. Now I know that a part of it is becoming a coconspirator.

One of the ways this approach was directly helpful to me, other than being able to answer the question of what people could do, was that I was able to bear a little bit of the weight. Or if not bear weight, at least act as a shield. What I witnessed was that what makes her much more tired or down or weary or whatever adjective you'd like to select is that people will ask her to explain the history of injustice in five minutes, or tell her to get over it, or avoid the subject of race altogether. This is not helpful! Or they'll ask her to contribute her time—for free—to some cause. They don't realize that a workshop on how to be less racist for a bunch of white people, led for free by Black people, is not at all helpful to those same Black people. The white people leave feeling better about themselves, whereas the Black facilitator leaves tired, having given up a night of relaxation for no pay. As a coconspirator, I could recommend books. I could share talking points, and I could provide action steps. Sometimes this meant saying no to things for her. Other times it was helping speak together. And it was always saying I see you and asking how are you doing. She was feeling major pain. Her friends were feeling major pain. Saying something like "I'm sorry" or asking "How are you doing?" would be much more helpful. Now I at least have an answer for my friends when they ask what they can do: become a coconspirator.

This might not be the direct or exact experience of your colleagues of color, but they are feeling something. Expressing this or asking questions can be very helpful.

The friends of ours who did this, by giving hugs, or kind words, or acts of kindness directly to Jess, were so appreciated. It can be awkward to express kindness or sympathy to someone because of what's going on in the national scene, but that awkwardness is okay, and it's a lot better to do something about it than not. —*Thomas Bratt*   ■ ▨ ■

I asked Tom to explain that shift because he and I do this E/D/I work in our own home. Thinking of yourself as a coconspirator can go a long way toward overcoming your fears. If someone says something harmful or incorrect about your best friends or family members, you come to their defense. You do so because you are on their side and to not step in would be harmful. Being a coconspirator is similar. You step in. It might help if you think of it like a relationship. Relationships that are healthy are active, whereas ones that are unhealthy are often toxic or stale. Healthy relationships deal with events as they happen and move on. Unhealthy relationships hide things or avoid them. In order to have a healthy relationship with diversity, it must be active. There have been countless situations in which we've had to talk through issues and share things. We both bring bias, and we both bring assumptions. At first, we held some things back, but now we're quite open and honest.

Even in our marriage, what stopped us was fear.

I'm going, in just a moment, to answer the most common questions I hear in my trainings, but first I want to pause and take a step back and answer one other question that seems to be just below the surface: What do I do if I made mistakes in the past, ignored issues of E/D/I, or am just now realizing how important anti-bias work is?

In addition to being important, the work of E/D/I and anti-bias training and racial justice is necessary. In the United States, and in a lot of the world, people have created systems that are unequal. Righting these wrongs takes work. Active work. For the sake of justice, we must fix it. We can fix this, too. One of my good friends, Mia Henry, is an expert in transformative justice. She conducts civil rights tours throughout the South. Seeing her work is witnessing beauty. She does a fantastic job of showing the past as it was, without apology, while also providing action steps on how to make amends. *This* is reconciliation. The goal of restorative justice is equality. The practice of E/D/I includes making amends if and when you make a mistake. Mia outlines how to do this in a three-step process:

1. Admit responsibility.
2. Express remorse.
3. Make amends.

This process can be big or small, public or private. To show what this process looks like in action, I have two personal stories of making amends.

A few years ago, my staff were going to do a *Let's Talk About Race in Storytimes* workshop at our local children's museum. When selecting books to show all different representations, I grabbed one with Asian American representation. Although I knew a lot about biases, stereotypes, and misrepresentations of the Black experience, I did not have that same grasp of knowledge about the Asian American identity. Someone pointed out that one of the books I selected portrayed a common stereotype. By choosing only that book, without that knowledge, and presenting it as cute or fun or correct, I would have been accidentally adding to that single story. I'm glad the mistake was pointed out to me. The presentation would have been innocent on my end but could have been damaging to the community. I made a mental note to be more intentional about book selections for representations I was less familiar with.

In 2017 I was asked to be on a panel at the American Library Association conference in Chicago. The goal of the panel was to talk about our experience of being minorities in the workplace. A Twitter post used to promote the event even stated that there would be "no white men speaking." The panel was all women—three were white, and two of us were Black. One of the white women had intentionally invited my colleague and me to join the panel to bring racial diversity. My name and the group I represented (Libraries4BlackLives) were used to attract people to the event, which was more than an hour long and highly attended. Shortly into the presentation, it became very obvious that my colleague of color and I were *only* brought in to provide diversity. In total, we spoke for ten minutes. When we were given a chance to speak, we had to split that time. At first I wondered what was going on. During the event I even double-checked to make sure I had submitted everything from my biography to slides in the time frame that was asked of me. I felt like I was there only because I'm a minority. It was awkward. People in the audience noticed. After the presentation was over, one of my friends who had been in attendance asked, "Why didn't she let you talk? Why did the white women dominate the conversation?" These situations are not okay, and for far too long they haven't been addressed.

Shortly after the conference, I expressed my concern to one of the people who had asked me to be on the panel. I explained how I felt, and why I felt that way. I did it not to shame her or make her feel bad, but to show how well-meaning people can actually do harm. Her intent was to be inclusive. Her impact caused isolation. She made amends. A few months later, she brought me to her state to do training for her staff, using my voice and experience to help talk about race in storytime. She used her mistake to take responsibility and, more importantly, to make amends. She moved from an ally to a coconspirator.

The thing that often gets in the way of standing up for justice is fear. To be more open, we have to be intentional. So let's look at how to be intentional in talking about race in a way that is productive, supportive, and collaborative. When it comes to overcoming their fears, people need reinforcement. I've included some suggestions in the text box "Steps to Success," but I'll also answer some of the questions that I often get in Q&As.

🔲🔲🔲 STEPS TO SUCCESS 🔲🔲🔲

- **Play Worst-Case Scenario.** What's the Worst That Can Happen? is a game that I like to play. I have been conscious as a Black professional that whatever choice I make can have enormous consequences—like losing my job. Before I started Libraries-4Black Lives, I would play a game that was really predicting the worst-case scenario. This game would help me role-play my response if I made a mistake or someone complained.
- **Accept that mistakes will happen.** Fear of saying the wrong things or causing an unintended offense does not mean that you should avoid talking about race. Apologize, and listen. "I am sorry that I said _____. Thank you for letting me know how that made you feel. I will take steps to do better. Is there anything I can do to make it right?" Use restorative practice questions to help you unpack what happened.
- **Model what inclusion looks like.** Be careful that you are not enforcing microaggressions with your words or thinking you are giving a compliment when in fact you are reinforcing a stereotype. Practice your approach ahead of time and make sure to practice it with others, too. Use positive language from this book. Remember, if you do say something that is offensive or disrespectful and a caregiver comes to talk to you, listen.
- **Practice.** Find a colleague who can provide support for engaging intentionally in this work. You cannot do this work alone. Just as you read a storytime book out loud before the storytime, practice talking about race at different storytime transitions to see where it fits best.

- **Have the tough conversations.** It is good to build skills in having tough conversations. Sometimes a follow-up conversation may be necessary, and it is okay to not have an answer on the spot.
- **Set a positive tone.** Sometimes it is not what you say, it is how you say it. If you talk about race in an uncomfortable manner, you are reinforcing that race is something to be avoided. That message can have an effect whether you are talking in your storytime space or with colleagues. If you are not comfortable discussing race, then no one around you will be.

Can White People Successfully Talk about Race?

The answer to this question is (and has to be) yes. The reality is that the library profession is 88 percent white. So white librarians will *have* to get comfortable talking about race with caregivers and young children, especially in the company of blackness, if we want a more equitable society. If you doubt your ability to do so, dive deep into identity and power and educate yourself on the roots of oppression. Talking about race cannot be done successfully without understanding identity, history, and power. We can't expect our children to grow up being more loving and kind without the tools and support to do so. (If you need help getting started, there are many resources, some listed in the back of this book. I encourage white librarians to listen to Heather McGhee's TED Talk, "Racism Has a Cost for Everyone."[1])

What if I am labeled as having an agenda or am accused of using taxpayer dollars to fund an agenda?

First, there is no agenda behind being a good citizen and wanting justice for all people. Second, our Constitution grants the rights to "life, liberty, and the pursuit of happiness" to all people. (But, as with the Constitution itself, it took action to include *all* people.) We tell children to "love everyone" and "treat everyone fairly," as if saying those words will somehow present a magical blueprint that gives kids the language, behavior, and tools to navigate identity biases. We have to model anti-bias behavior to kids. In order to do that, we have to be able to talk about bias in a healthy, age-appropriate way. (I suggest listening to Heather McGhee's talk, "How Can I Be a Better American?"[2]) If accusations persist, you can show your full range of programming, which typically includes a wide mix for all people.

How do I talk about race in storytime in a mixed or homogeneous setting?

If this is a concern of yours, it's probably a good idea to educate yourself. I provide a huge list of resources for educators in the appendix that are all great. There are so many great videos and podcasts. Dive in! And then, just try. Be yourself and just go for it. There are specific videos about why we are awkward in talking about race and how we often do so in a way to be casual and liked instead of giving the subject the respect it deserves. A *New York Times* video entitled "Why We're Awkward" highlights the term *racial anxiety* and discusses how knowing that it makes us feel a little weird gives us permission to lean into talking about race.[3]

How do I have tough conversations with caregivers?

I often equate this question to having a conversation about what is in our book collection or about library policy when caregivers want to complain about their kid checking out an item that the caregiver may deem inappropriate. Start by leaving your defensiveness at the door. Seek first to understand. Be prepared with talking points, and if the person tries to drag you into an emotional hurricane, do not waver. These conversations are also like any other skill—they take practice. And remember, you don't have to have all the answers. You can say things like "I don't know" or "I wasn't aware of that" or "I'm sorry." Honesty is a good policy.

What if I do not have institutional support?

I'll acknowledge that it's hard to make change without institutional support. But at the same time, change starts with one person—maybe that's you! If there are no talking points or language for staff to use when addressing E/D/I, then the effort will not be successful until someone decides to make it a big deal. If that someone is you, start by doing research. Once you have gathered information about what institutional support is needed, develop talking points and have a conversation with whomever you need to. Libraries are for the community—the entire community. Chances are, your mission and vision statements say this to some extent. If no one is doing E/D/I work, that's a great opportunity to start. You can start small and build from there. (I also provide a list of resources and go through this topic in chapter 5.)

How do I overcome my fear of talking about race?

Plainly, you just do. A mental shift to coconspirator is especially helpful here. If you have never talked about race before, you may have to battle through the fear. Next, seek out help and set realistic goals and time frames. Making sure that you are supported in this work is instrumental. If you have room in your budget, hiring a facilitator is very helpful. A day or two with an expert can help address a lot of talking points, outline acceptable terminology, and show you ways to begin the process. If you get this chance, take it very seriously and ask the questions you need to ask. If you have a fear of being fired, then this work is daunting and change will not happen. Making sure that fears are addressed is very important to engaging everyone in this work. If not, the well intended can come across as anti.

My spouse is white and middle class, and his family has a culture of silence. For them, it is much better to avoid a topic than it is to hurt someone's feelings. Consequently, they wait for someone to bring up something that is sensitive. In turn, many conversations that should have happened never do. The result is silence, and that silence is hard to interpret. Are you avoiding it? Are you against progress? He has been asked many times how I'm doing, or how political events have impacted me. These people think they're being kind and supportive, but the choice to ask him actually hurts the cause and isolates me. I'm like, why don't you ask me? For this one the answer is a resounding YES! Talk to your colleagues. They're feeling pain and have opinions and feelings and want you to acknowledge it.

I say this not to shame or blame but, rather, to point out how permeating some behavior can be. It might be scary, it might be a bit difficult or awkward or both, but your colleagues will feel a lot more comfortable if you ask them. But be sure to listen to their answers.

Creating Institutional Change

If you want to bring this work to a larger team, some work will be needed before you can create this change. Some of the following questions come from adapting a form of change management. Change management comes from the business world and is defined by Wikipedia as "a collective term for all approaches to prepare, support, and help individuals, teams, and organizations in making organizational change" (https://en.wikipedia.org/wiki/Change_management).

1. What is the reason for doing this work? If people do not understand the value, change will not happen.
2. What does success or failure look like? Is it just getting people to recognize authors of color and openly talking to families about these authors? Is it to engage in talking about race? How will you know if you are successful or if you failed?
3. What are the high- and low-level risks in doing this work?
4. What is the plan to mitigate those risks (e.g., by having talking points)?
5. Is this a solo endeavor, or will training be required? If the latter, how do you get everyone up to speed (e.g., shared language for social justice terms, book evaluations)?

What if my Black and Brown colleagues do not think this work is important?

Black people are not a monolith. My colleague Mia Henry says that Black people have long been united in our oppression, which often overlooks the diversity within our own identities. That's also why I use the game Trading Races (see chapter 1) to kick off the discussion. Like all people, Black and Brown people have thoughts and opinions ranging across the spectrum. They are allowed those opinions. It doesn't change the goal and shouldn't stop you!

Is it only my Black and Brown colleagues who can do this work?

No. Do not put the heavy lifting of this work on your Black and Brown colleagues. It is very important that you do not leave the work of E/D/I to just librarians of color. We've had to do it for too long. We're tired. When it comes to helping, the people of color are given any and all assignments of E/D/I way too often. This approach is not helpful. Whenever an event hits the mainstream media that deals with violence—Breonna Taylor, George Floyd, Alton Sterling, Philando Castile—people call on me to speak about it. They assume that because I'm Black and do E/D/I work, I'll have a statement right away. Then they ask me to talk about the event, which often means doing an interview, writing an article, or speaking on a podcast. Too often, the expectation is that I'll do this on my time, free of charge. This doesn't help me. It helps *them*. They can feel like they brought in an "expert" to explain things and that they've done something to help. But it leaves me tired. It is not on us. It is on *everyone*. All librarians need to help and do their part.

How to Talk to Your Colleagues about Race

I'm going to end this chapter by talking about *how* to talk to your colleagues. Before I created this tool kit, I remember establishing my personal standards—I would not shy away from topics, and I would gauge whether my staff could understand socially nuanced situations when dealing with the public. For example, when police violence became a national topic, I checked in with all my branch staff. We talked openly about what resources we had, what was needed, and how we would handle caregivers as we engaged in this work, whether the goal was to deescalate patron tensions or provide support for learning about what was happening.

Talking to your colleagues is very important in undertaking this work. A lot of conversations will be needed to gain support and buy-in from staff in order to move forward. These conversations are not for analysis-paralysis. Keep these goals in mind: to hear everyone's fears, to express empathy and validate concerns, to provide tools, and to move forward with an understanding of what this work will require (for example, doing work for E/D/I/ requires personal good health and well-being).

If you want the conversations to be beneficial, it helps to be intentional, making sure you ask whether this intention will give you the impact that you want. The most important thing after the conversations is to provide clarity about next steps. It is not enough to keep meeting. You need context for *doing*. This work should be intentional and thoughtful, not just haphazard. Make sure you have your shared agreements ready for the space. Use classroom guides to help calm strong emotions. For example, you could use a check-in system—such as the stoplight system or thumbs up/down—to see how everyone is doing in the conversation. If you have a budget, it may be helpful to bring in a facilitator (Mia Henry or Elon Cook Lee are two excellent choices). If you are facilitating, bring a lot of questions to help people process empathy. Learning for Justice (formerly Teaching Tolerance) has a guide and standards for educators that help in leading facilitations (see the "Facilitator Guides" page on the Learning for Justice website, https://www.learningforjustice.org).

It's also important to allow people time to process. Don't force people to talk. If the conversation is not going well verbally, ask people to write down their fears or issues. Remind people to breathe, and take time to communicate and understand that you can have hard conversations in an open setting without judgment. Know that you may learn things about your coworkers that are unexpected and that may need to be unpacked outside your work setting. Do not use your colleagues of color as a shield or harbinger of whatever form of justice you want from the conversation.

Another model to help facilitate conversation is the Conversation Café (www.conversationcafe.org/). Conversation Café has great, simple ground rules to ensure that everyone is heard and has a chance to talk.

Also, remember that, as when dealing with books, one experience does not represent the whole. What your colleague tells you is true for *them* and may not necessarily represent colleagues of color.

Bringing about a better world is up to us, one librarian reading one book to one group of kids. You can do it. If you're nervous, the next chapter will show you six different examples of what I do.

Advocacy Phrases

If a member of the public has a political or moral viewpoint, it is not good to argue with them. Remember your professionalism as a representative of the library.

Example Patron Comment: "It looks like the library is full of agendas. You want to start brainwashing kids early and sharing revisionist history. I do not want my kids to have anything to do with this."

Staff Response: "I definitely hear your concerns. We know that not all our events are the right fit for every family. Can I show you our [play area, computers, event brochure, movie section] instead?"

Here are some other tips and talking points to deal with these situations.

Tips for Handling Upset/Disappointed Patrons

- Affirm how the patron is feeling. "I hear how upset you are about this. We believe it is up to the caregiver to decide what is appropriate for their family."
- Remember, you do not need to take verbal abuse from anyone. In a calm tone say, "I cannot keep helping you if you continue to talk to me this way." Ask for help from a supervisor if needed.
- If the patron keeps getting angry and you cannot resolve their issue, direct them elsewhere. "I don't think that I am the right person to address your concerns. Let me find a supervisor for you to speak with."
- Although it may feel personal, the patron's anger or disappointment is not about you. It is about the situation. Try to remain calm and neutral when dealing with an upset patron. Keep your body language open, make direct eye contact, and speak in a pleasant but firm tone.

Other Advocacy Phrases

- "Our library has made a commitment to diversity, equity, and inclusion. We find that it is important to celebrate and affirm children's differences."

- "We want to help children become comfortable working, living, and communing alongside people who look different from themselves."
- "It is important that all kids see themselves reflected in stories. This helps them have the tools to be tolerant adults who can coexist with others."

○ ○ ○ SELF-REFLECTION ○ ○ ○

▶ Have you seen injustice play out in your library and stood idly by?

▶ What happened, and how did you feel?

▶ Have you witnessed an injustice that you did something about? What happened, and how did you feel?

▶ Have you seen an injustice and stepped in as a coconspirator? If so, how did that feel?

NOTES

1. Heather C. McGhee, "Racism Has a Cost for Everyone," filmed December 2019, TED video, 14:12, https://www.ted.com/talks/heather _c_mcghee_racism_has_a_cost_for_everyone?language=en.

2. Heather C. McGhee, "What Can I Do to Change? You Know? To Be a Better American?," interview, *Washington Journal*, C-Span, August 20, 2016, https://www.youtube.com/watch?v=BsUa7eCgE_U.

3. Saleem Reshamwala, "Why We're Awkward," *New York Times*, December 16, 2016, video, 2:41, https://www.nytimes.com/video/ us/100000004818673/why-were-awkward.html.

4

. . . .

MODELING THE WORK
Six Sample Storytimes

n order to talk about race in storytime, you have to have—*storytime!* Doing storytimes has always been one of my favorite parts of being a librarian. It's so fun to get kids excited about reading and watch them process the world. What I want to do here is show you what I do, using six great books as examples. These six books are only a starting point, and there are so many great books out there.

We all have different levels of experience, not only when it comes to E/D/I but also when it comes to conducting storytime. If you're new and starting off, it's fine to start small. If you've been doing storytimes for years and want to add anti-bias training, there's something for you as well.

All these books have worked very well for me. Feel free to use them. Let's get started!

Baby Sample Storytime

Storytime Space Introduction	• Music playing • Space for your sign-in (sheet and/or stickers), stamps for kids to take • Bubble machine blowing bubbles
Welcome Song	(Use a welcome song of your choice)
Introduction to the Space	• Overview and welcome • "Choo-Choo name song" (insert children's names; https://www.youtube.com/watch?v=gr4gtVYSAEg)
Song	"Well Hello Everybody, Can You Touch Your (Nose, Toes, Head, Tummy)?" (https://www.youtube.com/watch?v=utQDMQ2JVWs)
Song	(Use a song of your choice)
Activity	(Use an activity of your choice)
Rhyme	(Use a rhyme of your choice)
Rhyme	(Use a rhyme of your choice)
Parent Tip	Example comment: "When talking to your child, it is okay to point out racial differences."
Choral/ Shared Book	• Board book: *Whose Knees Are These?* by Jabari Asim. • For example, on a picture walk you might point out, "Look! This baby on the cover has brown skin."
Song	(Feel free to choose a singable song with motions of your choice)
Closing Song	(Use a closing song of your choice)
Free Play	Baby toys and music

Toddler Sample Storytime 1

Storytime Space Introduction	• Music playing • Space for your sign-in (sheet and/or stickers), stamps for kids to take • Bubble machine blowing bubbles
Opening Song/Rhyme	(Use an opening song or rhyme of your choice)
Introduction to the Space	Introduction to library, bathrooms, event highlights, etc.
Early Literacy Parent Tip	Repetition is important. Try to make sure that you sing or say the same rhyme or song at least three times. It will help the children get used to language and sentence structure.
Action Song	(Use an action song of your choice)
Action Song	(Use an action song of your choice)
Action Song/Rhyme	(Use an action song or rhyme of your choice)
Parent Tip	Respect your child's curiosity about the world around them by answering their hard and sometimes embarrassing questions. "Let me think about that for a while" or "That is a good question" or "I do not know" are great responses.
Book	*Woke Baby* by Mahogany L. Browne
Letter Tub/Puppet	• *W/w* for "window" or "web" • Pull items from a tub that sound like *w* or use a "w" puppet
Dance Song	Parachute Play (Use a song of your choice)
Choral/ Shared Reading	Example: *Giraffes Can't Dance* by Giles Andreae, illustrated by Guy Parker-Rees
Goodbye Song	(Use a song of your choice)

Toddler Sample Storytime 2

Storytime Space Introduction	• Music playing • Space for your sign-in (sheet and/or stickers), stamps for kids to take • Bubble machine blowing bubbles
Opening Song/Rhyme	(Use an opening song or rhyme of your choice)
Introduction to the Space	Introduction to instructor, library, bathrooms, event highlights, etc.
Early Literacy Parent Tip	Try to make talking, singing, reading, writing, and playing a part of your everyday routine. It's the best way to help children get ready to read.
Action Song	(Use an action song of your choice)
Action Song	(Use an action song of your choice)
Action Song/ Rhyme	(Use an action song or rhyme of your choice)
Parent Tip	While reading to your child, it is okay to point out racial differences. "Is that skin lighter or darker than your own?" "Did you know we can be born with different skin colors?" "The book that we are reading shows Black and Brown-skinned people. Isn't it great that we may be born different, but we all have a heart that beats with love for each other!"
Book	*My People* by Langston Hughes
Letter Tub/Puppet	*P/p* for "people," "peace," or "purple"
Dance Song 1	Parachute Play (Use a song of your choice)
Dance Song 2	(Use a song of your choice)
Choral/ Shared Reading	(Use a shared reading book of your choice)
Goodbye Song	(Use a goodbye song of your choice)
Activity	Create station

Family Sample Storytime

Introduction	• Music playing • Space for your sign-in (sheet and/or stickers), stamps for kids to take • Books for families to browse and read together
Welcome Song	(Use welcome song of your choice)
Introduction to Storytime Space	Introduction to library, event highlights, family bathrooms, parents, tips, etc.
Rhyme	(Use a rhyme of your choice)
Book	*I Got the Rhythm* by Connie Schofield-Morrison
Parent Tip	When talking to your child, it is okay to point out racial differences. "Look at her skin (or hair). Is it the same as or different from yours? Do you know that we are all born with different shades of skin colors (and hair textures)? Doesn't she have awesome afro puffs?"
Songs and Rhymes	(Use song and rhyme of your choice)
Song	(Use song of your choice)
Book	*Chicka Chicka Boom Boom* (with music) by Bill Martin Jr. and John Archambault, illustrated by Lois Ehlert
Songs/Rhymes with Props	(Select three songs that use shakers, scarves, drumsticks, etc.)
Closing Song	(Use a closing song of your choice)
Activity and/or Free Play	(Select your preferred closing activity)

Preschooler Sample Storytime 1

Storytime Setup	• Music playing • Space for your sign-in (sheet and/or stickers), stamps for kids to take • Books for caregivers to browse and read together
Opening Song	(Use an opening song of your choice)
Introduction	Introduction to the library, welcome song, etc.
Action Song	(Use an action song of your choice)
Action Song	(Use an action song of your choice)
Book	*Hands Up!* by Breanna J. McDaniel, illustrated by Shane W. Evans
Parent Tip	Share with your child your feelings about race when reading picture books. "Look at how they are all holding their hands up. We saw how this character uses their hands in many different ways. It makes me happy that groups of people can come together to use their hands to tell everyone what is important to them."
Calm Song	(Use a calming or quiet song of your choice)
Book	*This Is Not My Hat* by Jon Klassen
Goodbye Song	(Use a goodbye song of your choice)
Activity	Create signs about a social topic or national issue.

Preschooler Sample Storytime 2

Storytime Setup	• Music playing • Space for your sign-in (sheet and/or stickers), stamps for kids to take • Books for caregivers to browse and read together
Opening Song	(Use a welcome song of your choice)
Introduction	Introduction to the library, directions, etc.
Action Song	(Use an action song of your choice)
Parent Tip	When talking to your child, it is okay to point out racial differences.
Book	*What's the Difference?* by Doyin Richards. "Empathy is an important skill for growing up. We can learn from others about our wonderful differences by listening like these kids are doing here (mimic holding ear out to listen). Can you listen?"
Calm Song	(Use a calming song of your choice)
Book	*Hooray for Hat* by Brian Won
Drumstick Song	(Use a drumstick song of your choice)
Parachute Play	(Use a parachute play song of your choice)
Goodbye Song	(Use a goodbye song of your choice)
Activity	Provide a create station (random assortment of supplies) for preschoolers to create a story. Ask them to share with their caregiver(s) the story that they made and have them take turns listening to stories that other kids have made.

BUILDING YOUR PRACTICE

n the preceding chapters, we looked at theory and talked through ideas and fears. This chapter is intended to help you build your practice of how to talk about race in storytimes in a positive way. When I facilitate workshops, I like to incorporate time for the participants to think through their practice, but more than that, I like to give them an opportunity to use what I've presented and give them time to plan and prepare. So let's do that now.

I often find that talking about race brings up a lot of different feelings for a lot of people. There's a full range of emotions and experience and tension. Some people have been on the receiving end of systemic racism for years but have never admitted or realized it. For them, this work brings up a lot of pain. This work gives language to what they are feeling. Some people get really emotional. Other people think we should just move on and deny the existence of any oppression. They say that it's in the past and that people should get over it. We're all at different points in our journey. You might have to sit with it before you can move on. I've also worked with people who want to get going but have no idea where to start. And also with people who are very well meaning, but their entire group shares a single story, so they don't know *how* to start. I've worked with groups that are already taking great steps toward doing this work but need a guide. We're all in it together. With practice, you can get there.

I think of this work like music.

When you learn an instrument, you need to *practice*. If your goal is to play a piece of music well, you must focus on each note before you can play the entire piece. In music it doesn't matter where you start, it's how you practice.

I found an interesting exercise called "How Diverse Is Your Universe?"[1] In the exercise, participants are given a cup and a bunch of beads of various colors. The facilitator poses a series of scenarios, such as "The neighbors on either side of my house are _____," and participants place a bead representing that skin color into the cup. This exercise explores entertainment, places of worship, health, places of recreation, and choices of film and music. At the end, participants look at their cup and see how "diverse" their universe is. The results are eye-opening for a lot of people.

Often, the minorities have a cup with all different colors of beads, but the white participants have a cup with mostly white beads. If you're a minority, you have to interact with a lot of people and cultures. It's often the white participants who live in a monolithic group. Much of white America sees, and interacts with, only people who look like they do. Realizing this limited experience can elicit strong reactions. People begin waking up to the fact that it's really easy to spend time with people who look and think just like they do.

Think about your normal routine. When it comes to interacting with your neighbors, peers, friends, or spiritual leaders or with those in positions of authority, how diverse is the group? In your daily interactions—phone, text, e-mail, social media—*who* are you interacting with? When thinking through a life decision, or soliciting advice or wisdom, do you reach out to people who are of a different race, religion, or socioeconomic level?

If you find that your universe looks a lot alike, a great first step is to acknowledge that limitation and then you can do things to change it. Your second step could be as simple as visiting a museum, restaurant, or store that you wouldn't normally go to. It could be watching a movie or documentary about other cultures, or listening to different music. Of extra importance is that children notice if the things and people in their books—and in real life—are similar or different. Do their caregivers see all different types of people throughout the day, or does their caregivers' entire network look the same? If the network looks the same, does this network normalize behaviors by praising their own as superior? One way to combat this limitation would be to intentionally diversify your world. (The TV shows *Black-ish*, *United Shades of America*, and *Taste the Nation* are great starts.) A more equitable society stems from all of us doing our part to realize that everyone is equal. Every voice is special and unique, and we can see and appreciate these voices.

One of the ways to think of anti-bias practices in the storytime space is in terms of community building. Silvia Cristina Bettez writes, "Community building can be a way of enacting social responsibility towards others. . . . [C]ommunity not only could be, but should be, based on interdependence between diverse individuals and centralize appreciation of differences."[2] A good early step toward building a welcoming storytime space is to think about what community partners your library engages with. Ask these questions: Are we interacting with different community groups and members? Are these partners diverse? Are these partners being represented in storytime? When I first got to my library, one of the things I noticed was that a lot of our community was missing from the storytime space. To do so, I had to comb through a lot of the different organizations in my city that were doing things but were not necessarily collaborating and put them in touch with one another. Relationship building is also a good way to do this outreach.

It can help if you think of the United States as a mosaic instead of a melting pot. A lot of kids have been taught that the United States is a melting pot, which meant that once you come to this land, you are now American and must assimilate. That assimilation was then celebrated. If we think in terms of a mosaic instead, we can keep our individual culture and diversity and celebrate the uniqueness while *adding* to the whole.

Libraries, and our storytimes, are one of the best places to celebrate the mosaic that is America. Libraries are one of the few spaces that are diverse and where we can really focus on this quality. Knowledge is power, and access to knowledge is the gateway to that power. Which, in some ways, is the whole point of the library. Representation matters and is so empowering for the children in your community. Changing the melting pot narrative is imperative, and showing a diverse cast of authors can really help change that narrative. Storytime is perfect for this work.

When talking about race in storytime, remember that there are entry steps to this work. You do not have to come out of the gate talking about cultural identities if you do not have the skill to do that. When you conduct a storytime, you're helping children grow and learn, and a part of that education is to notice and recognize differences in people and skin tones. It's totally fine—and great—to point out these differences, which the kids notice anyway. I will repeat that you can work your way up by starting to read about different lived experiences, telling caregivers about awards based on those experiences, and then thoughtfully figuring out how to build up to being able to talk about race in an open, age-appropriate way. This process is done through affirmation. (Refer to the affirmations at the end of chapter 2.)

It can be difficult to navigate the innocent questions of children in a society, like the United States, that values independence and personal opinion and free speech. In a society that has had to have major disruptions in the law—the Civil Rights Act, the Americans with Disabilities Act, the Marriage Equality Act—to make things equal. We have this deep-rooted belief that all are entitled to their opinion, and because we don't want to offend, we often don't talk. This silence is how bias is created. *Anti-bias is a practice.* One does not learn unless one makes mistakes.

Children are much more resilient, and much better at handling difference, than many adults give them credit for. It is not they who place bias or negativity on differences; rather, it is adults who do so. Adults do it because of the way they have been trained, through what they were told was normal. If the starting point is that one race or sexual orientation or culture is below another race or sexual orientation or culture, that will shape how children think about and see the world. But there are some ways that we should let the children be the guide. Children don't bring a bias to differences—that bias is taught. If we do this work in a positive way, answering questions and celebrating beauty, we can change the world.

It takes skill to do this work. If you start talking about race without practicing or shaping it into your work, then you will not be able to respond to uncomfortable situations. When it comes to fears about pushing a "liberal" narrative or pushing an agenda, look at the totality of your storytimes, rather than at one at a time.

When I began to formalize this work, there were concerns that storytimes would not be fun anymore or that parents would think that there was an "agenda" beyond just trying to get kids to love differences.

But these are adult fears, fears they project onto kids. Talking about race in storytime can fit into the beautiful disaster of a storytime space for any age group. It can be as easy as pointing out differences when they come up or showcasing different representations in your storytime planning. No one is saying to exclude white families or white men. No one is saying to have only families of color or families that fall on the LGBTQ spectrum or families with different levels of ability. When a taboo topic comes up, body language is important. Most people are waiting for the worst and do not know how to respond. A lot of caregivers tend to shut conversations down, or parents of color are expecting someone to say something disrespectful. Furthermore, all parents struggle with discomfort if their child points out what they may consider a "disturbing observation" like "Why is their skin dark?" or "Why do they have yarn in their hair?" Such questions can lead to uncomfortable situations. This discomfort comes from parents' bias, rather than from kids' understanding or empathy. When children ask questions such as "Why is her skin black?" or "Why is he in a wheelchair?" or "Why do your mom and dad look different?" or "Why do you have two dads?" or any such question that a child asks innocently, a lot of Americans have a tendency to tense up.

If you feel a little nervous, or question yourself, one thing to keep in mind as you prepare is that the families in your community look to you as an expert on how to model anti-bias in their homes. Embrace that role. When you give a storytime, caregivers are there partly for you to show them what they can also do. That purpose can be fun and empowering.

Another technique that helps if you're unsure of what to say is to embrace the "I don't know." In one of my reference interview trainings, we were taught that librarians should never outright say no. If a child asks you a question that you do not know the answer to, one very good response is "That's a great question. Let's look it up!" Doing so allows you to be a helper on the path to knowledge, while subtly showing that knowledge is a process. A lot of time if there is a tricky research question, we may not be able to figure out the answer right away, but there are plenty of experts with all types of skills that can help us solve a puzzle. I loved research puzzles and used to look forward to the calls from patrons who were trying to find a book or movie from their youth that they wanted to pass on to their own children. They might only remember one character's name or one episode from the show and then we'd go through my pal Google and find it. I look at research as something fun. Finding the book, movie, or TV show was a reward. Sometimes a patron only knew that the book had "a teddy bear in it" or that the "cover had someone in a gray hoodie." At other times, the request could be as arcane as "that one show that aired last week that had this important guest who talked about baseball."

If we can demonstrate this strategy in our storytimes, as storytime instructors, we can help empower parents to know that knowledge is a process. That is an extra special part that as librarians we can pass on to our storytime attendees. They do not have to fear social identities but can embrace that they might not have all the answers all the time and that they can do the research so they can follow up to make sure their child can respectfully interact with children of other identities. If you can communicate that you don't know all the answers but are committed to trying to find them, you're also showing attendees that you're a safe person to ask questions of. If someone asks you a question one week, you can always bring it up the next. That commitment can also show that you're actively learning, too.

I say this because when it comes to facts about the moon or the stars or animals, librarians do this research, but when it comes to things like diversity or how society operates, a lot of people don't like to admit that they don't know. Take the same attitude toward those issues. If a kid asks you a question, it is fine to respond that you don't know and that you'll figure it out together. Racial terminology about different identities is constantly changing, and it is okay to encourage caregivers that they can ask to make sure they are presenting identities accurately. Something you don't want to do is thwart a child's imagination or stop their questions—especially because they know what's going on.

Think, Plan, Do

When it comes to talking about race in storytime, it helps to be intentional. I think of this process as Think, Plan, Do! Before planning out your storytime, you need to *think* about placement of talking about race. Next, you need to *plan* out how you're going to talk about it. Then, *do* it!

Think

First, think about whether you will be talking about race at the beginning of storytime. This approach would give attendees a heads-up about what will be happening during your storytime session. You could say, "Welcome everyone! During these twelve weeks I will be reading books representing all different types of families that make up our wonderful community." Or "I will be showing representations of our diverse community and highlighting wonderful authors throughout this session."

In many of our storytimes at my library, we have everything set up ahead of time and the songs written out so everyone can see them. Before starting, we give a quick spiel—where to validate parking, what programs are coming up. This could be a good time to introduce race. Maybe you want to just talk about BIPOC authors throughout your storytime session. You can choose to highlight picture books from book lists or award nominees and explain why there are specific awards celebrating different picture book collections. Having these books and lists accessible to your patrons is also very helpful.

Choosing books to use for curriculum for your storytimes is a great time to begin the work of E/D/I. A great first step to talking about race is to showcase a collection of books by diverse authors: "There are a lot of great books out there, so check them out from our library or buy them from your local bookstore." It's important to highlight authors of different races and cultures and to be intentional about selecting those authors. This intentionality extends to, and is more obvious to see in, the characters found in the books. The kids will notice, so take some time to make sure the characters represent a wide range of people.

If you don't know many authors of color, use winners and finalists from awards like the Coretta Scott King Book Award or the Pura Belpré Award or the Asian/Pacific American Award for Literature or the American Indian Youth Literature Award—these are all good starting points. A plus of using award books is that they have been through a rigorous vetting process and have been deemed excellent by a committee that knew the importance of the award.

If you feel that you want to directly engage caregivers about race, think about how you will do that. What is your goal? What is your point? Are you trying to show a specific identity that is centered by the plot of the book, like *Let the Children March* by Monica Clark-Robinson or *I Am Every Good Thing* by Derrick Barnes? Are you trying to feature a book in which identity is not integral to the plot, like *Grandma's Tiny House* by JaNay Brown-Wood or *Ta-Da!* by Kathy Ellen Davis? Maybe you want to feature a picture book that helps educate caregivers about racial identity (*I, Too, Am America* by Langston Hughes and illustrated by Bryan Collier or *The Undefeated* by Kwame Alexander). You have to first think about what you are trying to present and whether it will be featured in the present or past. From there you want to make sure you have done all your background research so that you will present the book with the respect the identity deserves.

Plan

Next is planning. All storytime professionals have an outline (whether you are a veteran and have it memorized or a newbie and are still writing out your "storytime lesson plan"). When you shape your storytime plan, think about where the racial talking point tip works best for your audience and your book. Sometimes the tip works right at the start as an introduction, whereas at other times it would be good to make those connections at the end.

Remember when you were first learning how to memorize everything as a new storytime teacher? You might have learned songs by singing them under your breath at the public service desk or in your spare time at home. Either way, you had to practice. Similarly, you will have to practice how to say the racial talking point and build that skill in different ways until it does not detract from the overall storytime and you feel confident and comfortable celebrating differences. (You can always practice with your colleagues as well.) It is important to allow yourself a test run and practice to make sure you are comfortable talking through these points. Our storytimes are rife with diversity because of the songs and books we choose and who shows up in our space. I would argue that we are beyond the "identity crisis" that librarians have been debating about for a number of years and need to shift to defining how libraries can take a leading role, "using the fundamental concept that knowledge is created though conversation."[3] People now know that February is Black History Month, and it's good to celebrate the feats of African Americans. However, what can happen is that people will maybe take an interest for a little bit of that month and then nothing for the rest of the year.

When it comes to building a practice, one thing that may help is making sure that storytime itself is a priority.

A lack of representation can also happen in a way that is quite unintentional. Librarians can be busy, and unprepared, and then push a single narrative. A lot of times (pre-pandemic), storytimes were rushed and almost second nature to veterans. Often, we use books that are familiar and easy to access. (Maybe we use things we've used for years.) Sometimes we're busy and focus on one session at a time; as a result, we show only one story.

At my library, our storytimes are often eight or ten weeks long. We begin by looking at the entire session and having one theme or time or set of activities, and then plan it out from there. We don't want to do the same songs or activities every week. Doing so would get boring, and people wouldn't come back. So we switch it up and do an arts and crafts activity one week and drawing the next. We play a game the week after that and do a puzzle the next. We vary the program so that the kids have new, fun things to look forward to. You can do this same thing with the books. What I'm suggesting is that you think through the length of the storytime and make sure that you vary your programs to avoid the single story.

Do

Finally, it is time to do! You have thought about the importance of your book choice and about how you want to present the talking point, and you have practiced it. Now it is time to calm your nerves as best you can and get ready to present your program in front of a live audience. You will have to build skills in reading your audience, making direct eye contact, and not saying any more or less than what needs to be articulated at the moment.

After you finish, one very important part of daily practice is to incorporate reflection and evaluation—but not the scary kind! In the worksheets found in the "Conclusion" section of this book, you can put together an evaluation for the E/D/I framework. This is when you get to use it. Depending on how you personally work, your evaluation can be more open-ended or more focused. In my department, we have an evaluation that is very transparent and is given to all storytime leaders before they start the first session. It's built into the fabric of our department. We use it as a verbal self-reflection, post-storytime. I allow my librarians space to talk through what went well and what didn't. The evaluation sheet is available for everyone to look at any time and is the starting point of conversation. Having it gives us a conversation starter, something to talk about, and a goal to work toward. We use it to make things better. As Shuri says in *Black Panther*, "Just because something is good doesn't mean it can't be improved."

Assessing Storytime Books Using an E/D/I Lens

In order to build out your practice, you will need tools. I created an assessment framework to help when picking out storytime books. Every book is not going to have *everything*. Please do not overreact when you first see the framework. This is a guide to help you realize that when selecting storytime books, we have to decide within the general criteria of what makes a picture book have that "storytime appeal." You can find these criteria in the *Every Child Ready to Read* tool kit and other such materials about developmentally appropriate books for pre-reading. Additionally, when we talk about cultural representation of identities, we need to know that there are criteria for that as well. The following lists show general criteria for choosing a book for storytime.

Type of Story and Age Group

- Big-Book Length: words per page/number of pages
- Digital Story Pictures
- Oral Appeal: rhyming
- Other Interactivity: repetition of sounds/phrases

Content of the Book

- Is it scary?
- Is it hard to understand?
- Do the pictures connect with the text?

Applying an E/D/I Lens

1. Does this book provide a diversity of thoughts, ideas, opinions, perspectives, and experiences?
2. Does this book provide representation of diversity in gender, race, ethnicity, age, experiences, and so on?
3. Does this book provide the opportunity for participants to engage with and meet characters who are different and may express themselves differently?
4. Who is present in this book? Who will this book reach?
   - Will this book celebrate or affirm a storytime audience?
   - Will this book show language or cultural differences?
5. Who is missing in this book?
6. Is there an assumed awareness or expectation of children?
   - Expectation of community or children in a certain school system?
   - Expectation of community or children at a certain income level?
7. Does this book present a shared cultural value such as common experience?
   - What are the competing values and systems in this book?
8. Does this story present different families or represent only a social issue?
   - If it presents historical material, is the story accurate or does it insinuate a romanticized past?
   - Does the book represent feelings of superiority/inferiority in children?
9. How are the illustrations presented?
   - Are they engaging or caricature-like?
   - Do they misrepresent racial features (e.g., Asians with yellow skin)?

As of yet, there is no formalized or standardized structure for E/D/I tools. Creatively, you can mix and match tools from a variety of work that other organizations are doing. I would recommend checking out Project READY, Kirkus Collections, EmbraceRace, Teaching for Change, and the Brown Bookshelf. Part of this work is building out time to explore these tools. It is not enough to just have them written down. You must take the time to research, brainstorm, remember. Think. Plan. Do!

GREAT DIVERSE READ-ALOUDS, AGES 0–5

Maybe Something Beautiful:
How Art Transformed a Neighborhood
BY F. ISABEL CAMPOY AND THERESA HOWELL

This vibrant book has nice pictures, an interactive text, and portrayals of different community members, all revolving around the theme of art. The notes at the end add a layer of connection to the actual neighborhood the events happened in.

Mae Among the Stars
BY RODA AHMED

With deep hues of purple and blue mimicking space, this book has nice illustrations and sparse text. Within the book is nice intersectionality between race and gender.

Grandma's Tiny House
BY JANAY BROWN-WOOD

There's so much to unpack with *Grandma's Tiny House*. There are counting and hidden insects and pets throughout every page and, more importantly, space to show that sometimes you can be in spaces where everyone looks like you . . . and for the dominant culture, sometimes you can be in spaces where people do not look like you.

GREAT DIVERSE BOOKS, NOT GREAT READ-ALOUDS, AGES 0–5

Hammering for Freedom: The William Lewis Story
BY RITA L. HUBBARD

Great portrayal of the enslaved narrative. As a story-time selection, the text is too small and there are too many words per page to capture the attention of a toddler.

Out of Wonder: Poems Celebrating Poets
BY KWAME ALEXANDER, CHRIS COLDERLEY,
AND MARJORY WENTWORTH

A whole bunch of poems with darling illustrations, this book was the 2018 Coretta Scott King Book Awards Illustrator Winner. Unfortunately, at this developmental stage, you would not be reading poems from a giant book, especially if they are not the interactive type.

Memphis, Martin, and the Mountaintop
BY ALICE FAYE DUNCAN

A great portrayal of Martin Luther King's Sanitation Strike of 1968. Unfortunately, the nuance and subtext of this particular civil rights event are too sophisticated for toddler or preschool age.

STORYTIME APPEAL, TERRIBLE CULTURAL REPRESENTATION, AGES 0–5

So Tall Within:
Sojourner Truth's Long Walk Toward Freedom
BY GARY D. SCHMIDT

The artwork by Daniel Minter grounds this work heavily. Unfortunately, the language used within this work makes the enslaved narrative seem almost nonexistent because of the overused phrase "In Slavery Time." The subtleness of language creates the impression that slavery time could have happened in a different time instead of right here on Earth in America a few centuries ago.

A Fine Dessert: Four Centuries, Four Families, One Delicious Treat
BY EMILY LOCKHART

A terrible view that subtly romanticizes slavery. A mother and daughter moment of love that conquers all on the plantation? Books help reinforce the narratives that "slavery wasn't that bad" and that Blacks were inferior because "they would have done something about it if they didn't like it." There is no Black resistance portrayed in this narrative—just a passive acceptance of their circumstances.

Natalie's Hair Was Wild!
BY LAURA FREEMAN

Black women's hair is heavily politicized. Although the dominant culture will think that wild, curly hair doesn't matter, Black girls often are sent home from school and Black women are fired from their jobs and outlawed in government positions because of how they wear their hair. Hair is a sensitive topic because of the oppressive nature of cultural representations and needs to be handled with care when portrayed in storytime.

Shared Goals and Assessment

Doing the work outlined in this book will help you and your staff assess your starting point. If you know your collection is okay at representation, then maybe your staff members need more work regarding a shared E/D/I language. Maybe you did a diversity audit course and one about E/D/I, so then start with understanding how decolonization of children's literature will help you understand cultural representation in books.

Having goals to work toward helps in making sure that you are always building knowledge and creating a shared learning environment to make sure you are actively doing this work. If this work is important to you, then learning how to make sure you are portraying cultures in the most positive light is very important.

ooo SELF-REFLECTION ooo

> How do you choose what picture books to use in a session?

> Do you meet as instructors to discuss storytime books? How do you know which ones are the best to use for different age groups?

> Do you have support staff doing storytimes? How do they know what books to pick and how to shape their storytimes? How would this information work in relation to adding training?

> How do you select cultural representation in storytime books? How often do you purchase books for all storytime instructors, making sure diversity is accessible in your system for everyone?

> What do you know about decolonization of children's literature?

> Do you know who in the field is doing work related to decolonization of children's literature?

NOTES

1. University of Houston, Center for Diversity and Inclusion, "How Diverse Is Your Universe?," *Diversity Activities Resource Guide*, https://www.uh.edu/cdi/diversity_education/resources/_files/_activities/diversity-activities-resource-guide.pdf.
2. Silvia Cristina Bettez, "Critical Community Building: Beyond Belonging," *Educational Foundations* 25, no. 3–4: 3–19 (Summer–Fall 2011), https://files.eric.ed.gov/fulltext/EJ954978.pdf. Originally a keynote address at the conference of the Southeastern Association of Educational Studies, February 18, 2011.
3. R. David Lankes, *The Atlas of New Librarianship* (MIT Press, 2011), https://davidlankes.org/new-librarianship/the-atlas-of-new-librarianship-online/.

CONCLUSION
Championing the Work!

The *whole* point of learning how to talk about race is to *celebrate* differences. Audre Lord said, "It is not our differences that divide us, it is our inability to recognize, accept and celebrate our differences."[1] Race should not be a taboo topic, but because of the laws, policies, fear, intolerance, and traumatic baggage of our history, it is a taboo topic. Kids should be able to start learning empathy and tolerance at a young age by understanding how to talk about racial differences and learning how to respect other cultures and history. In order to do that with adults, I have to take everyone on a journey to either relieve their trauma or open up their worldview to leave that baggage behind so that they can celebrate differences, disrupt stereotypes and biases, and give children the tools to help them become better humans.

I leave you with this—you need to be a dreamer. If you do not have a big imagination, then the world will just stay as is. What's your dream regarding storytime inclusion? What are you already doing well? What do you need to do, and, ultimately, how will you advocate for this work at your library?

Good luck. You can do this, and we can make the world better one storytime at a time!

Storytime Action Plan

Name:
_____

Storytime Session Length (e.g., six weeks, twelve weeks): _____
_____

Storytime Session Age: _____
_____

Theme/Unthemed: _____
_____

What is my biggest fear? _____
_____

Beginner Challenge

How many books written and/or illustrated by POC will I highlight to my storytime attendees?_____

What parent tips can I convey that will help parents understand that talking about race is important? _____

Intermediate Challenge

Book title: _____

Author/Illustrator: _____

Storytime age: _____

Race and/or ethnicity featured: _____

What physical difference will I affirm? _____

What wording will I use? _____

What parent talking point will be featured? _____

Have I practiced my talking point with myself or others?   Yes /No

What was the outcome after my session? Did anyone comment? Did I debrief with colleagues? _____

Advanced Challenge

Write your direct observation each time you feature a parent tip or model talking about race.

Did anyone approach you for feedback or discussion? _____

How are you feeling about modeling inclusion? _____

_____

_____

_____

Who was present in your storytime? Who was missing? _____

_____

_____

_____

What resources can you use to help find picture books of POC if you are doing a themed storytime? _____

_____

_____

_____

Historical Challenge

I will read, watch, or listen to two nonfiction narratives about the history of laws and policies related to systemic oppression.

Date started: _____

Date completed: _____

Let's Talk About Race in Storytimes Ultimate Challenge

- I have successfully used all five talking tips with a homogeneous audience and a mixed audience.
- I have successfully done a picture walk featuring another race (e.g., Latinx, Asian American, etc.).

NOTE

1. See Lavelle Porter, "Dear Sister Outsider: On Audre Lorde and Writing Oneself into Existence," Poetry Foundation, May 18, 2016, https://www.poetryfoundation.org/articles/89445/dear-sister-outsider.

APPENDIX
Recommended Resources

Reading

Published Books

A Few Red Drops, Claire Hartfield

Anti-bias Education for Young Children and Ourselves, Louise Derman-Sparks and Julie Olsen Edwards, with Catherine M. Goins

Incidents in the Life of a Slave Girl, Harriet Jacobs

Invisible Man, Got the Whole World Watching: A Young Black Man's Education, Mychal Denzel Smith

NurtureShock: New Thinking about Children, Po Bronson and Ashley Merryman

So You Want to Talk About Race, Ijeoma Oluo

The Warmth of Other Suns, Isabel Wilkerson

We Are Not Yet Equal, Carol Anderson

What If All the Kids Are White? Anti-bias Multicultural Education with Young Children and Families, Louise Derman-Sparks, Patricia Ramsey, and Julie Olsen Edwards

World Wide Web

"Talking with Kids about Race and Racism at Oakland Public Library," *Webjunction* (https://www.webjunction.org)

Everyday Diversity (http://everydaydiversity.blogspot.com/)

"100 Race-Conscious Things You Can Say to Your Child to Advance Racial Justice," *Raising Race Conscious Children* (http://www.race conscious.org/)

"Talking to Kids about Race," by Lindsey Krabbenhoft, *Jbrary* (https://jbrary.com/)

"Talking to Kids about Race," *The Lakeshore Ethnic Diversity Alliance* (https://ethnicdiversity.org/programs/ttkar/)

"Vocational Awe and Librarianship: The Lies We Tell Ourselves,"
by Fobazi Ettarh, *In the Library with the Lead Pipe* (https://www
.inthelibrarywiththeleadpipe.org/)

Watching

"3 Ways to Speak English." Ted.com
"Amend: The Fight for America." Netflix
"Barbie and Nikki Discuss Racism | Barbie Vlogs." Youtube.com
"Color Blind or Color Brave." Ted.com
"Coming Together: Standing Up to Racism." CNN/Sesame Street
Racism Townhall, CNN.com
"How to Teach Kids to Talk about Taboo Topics." Ted.com
"The Danger of a Single Story." Ted.com

Listening

"Same Same Different," *Michigan Radio*
"The Invisibility of White Privilege," *Speaking of Psychology*
"The Problem We All Live With," *This American Life*
"White Parents Need to Talk to Their Kids about Race," *The Takeaway*

Equity, Diversity, and Inclusion Educators

Elon Cook Lee, director of interpretation and education in the Historic
Sites Department at the National Trust for Historic Preservation
Mia Henry, founder of Freedom Lifted

INDEX